Make your

dreams a reality

Unmasking
The Torch Bearer

Awakening the Light within You

Steven D. Morrison

Author of
In Spite Of …
Understanding the Motivation in Obstacles

Wasteland Press
Shelbyville, KY USA
www.wastelandpress.net

Unmasking the Torch Bearer
Awakening the Light within You
by Steven D. Morrison

First Printing—March 2009
978-1-60047-280-0
www.stevendmorrison.com

Printed in the U.S.A.

This book is dedicated to you—my cherished audience.
Because of you, I possess a voice in my writing that you desire to hear.

CKNOWLEDGMENTS

Foremost, I give my warmest thanks to God. Truly, it is my duty to extend my sincerest thanks to every person that has come into my life and functioned as a light for me. Out of love, I would like to thank my cherished family for all of their love and support: my mother, Betty R. Morrison; my grandmother, Rosa M. McShan; my darling niece, Bria Morrison; my aunt, Sandra Rancher; and my cousins Nicole Royston, April Royston, Bonita Carter, and Sarah T. Marshall.

I'm so thankful to have the unconditional love and support of my NIU family: Dr. Albert J. Holmes, Jr., Kenya Moss, Charles Morris, and James McGruder. I extend a special thanks to Sharrel Tillman and Neiresha Tate for their dutiful efforts toward organizing and managing my book tour.

In the spirit of achievement, I extend a special thanks to my fraternity brothers of Kappa Alpha Psi Fraternity, Incorporated and my chapter, College Park Alumni, who have provided me with love, support, and guidance: Craig Waters, Ed Swain, James Kates, Benjamin Cummings, Charles Morgan, Greg Mitchell, Dedrick Brown and Honorable Kwame T. Thompson. Honorable Hilton Miller, who consistently hosts book signings and utilizes my books as supplemental resources for his classroom instruction. I'm overwhelmed with joy by the gracious effort of Jabarr Lassley who wrote, arranged, and performed the song "Unmasking the Torch Bearer," to commemorate the publication of this book. Truly, the bonds of Phi Nu Pi continue to unite us now and forever.

Words cannot express how thankful I am to those who proudly promoted my work in the public domain: Kesha Monks and Kiss 98.7 FM, *The Sandi Sam Show,* Pam Osbey, and *The Literary Pizzazz Show.* To add to this, I would like to thank Sheryl Key and the Nu Lambda Omega Chapter of Alpha Kappa Alpha Sorority, Incorporated. It is a pleasure and an honor to thank Rene Patterson, Elaine Matthews, Michelle Brown, Bruce Brown, Lori Brown, Wanda

Drauhon, Valeri Eckles, Bridgette Jacobs, Cheryl Ashe, Kevon Windom, Alicia Jones, Rosetta Grima, Brian Fuller, Jerome Burnette, Maddie Tate, Mrs. Allen, and the St. Phillips A.M.E. Church Bookstore.

I would also like to thank the wonderful organizations who have subscribed to the services of Artemis Consulting Group and who now utilize my books for their youth programs: Sharon Higgs and Brian Perry and the Trio Program at Morehouse College; Paulette Saunders and the Trio Program at Georgia Southern University; and Sherontae Maxwell and the Talent Search Program at the University of Georgia.

I extend a very warm thanks to the flight attendants, gate agents, and management team at Delta Air Lines.

It is truly a pleasure and an honor to acknowledge my high school, Belleville Township High School East, and the faculty and staff for their support: Mr. Kniepkamp, Mrs. Phillips, and a very special thanks to my former English teacher, Mrs. Hoffmann, who planted a seed in me to write by acknowledging my talent for writing as a student.

In addition, I would like to thank the following people and organizations for generously hosting book signings: Hope Cranford and the Trio Program at Savannah State University; Natarielle Powell and Savannah Technical College; Janet and Sebastian Sherod and the Smoothie Café; Mary Smith, Paula Johnson, and the entire staff at St. Clair Associated Vocational Enterprises; LaGonda and Jayden McGruder; The House of Color; and Monica Fodderingham and the Atlanta-Fulton County Public Library System.

TABLE OF CONTENTS

PREFACE

Three years ago, my life changed significantly when I introduced my first book, *In Spite Of ...* In writing this book, I came to understand that I answered a call to duty that God directed into my life. I realized that God placed me on a path carved exclusively for me. This was first evidenced when I witnessed the high school students in the Upward Bound Program at Savannah State University execute the first theatrical production of *In Spite Of ...* To add to this, three colleges informed me of how my book functions as a timeless resource for classroom instruction.

As I reflect upon the numerous text messages, e-mails, and words of encouragement that I have received from members of my newly developed audience, my motivation heightens in regard to making a difference in this world through my writing.

In conjunction with any meaningful journey, I have definitely taken many steps forward, but also a few backward. Through it all, words cannot articulate or capture the overall magnificence of this phenomenal journey. I have also answered a call from you, my beloved audience, to continue to write.

Unmasking the Torch Bearer provides functional evidence of how our journey through life encompasses gingerly docking on the shores of happiness, becoming immersed in the tides of anger, and experiencing the still of defeat and dismay, as well as indulging in the draft of sorrow. Nonetheless, through each of these meaningful experiences, there is a light that can be illuminated. From this, we are granted the opportunity to maximize on our greatness. With this in mind, it is up to each of us to discover how to ignite the spiritual light that functions as our guide.

As you journey through each chapter of this book, it is my hope that you will capture an understanding of how this book functions as a signature to document the power of the charismatic dynamism that resides in each of us. It is with great pleasure, humility, and fortitude that I introduce *Unmasking the Torch Bearer* to you. Enjoy!

CHAPTER 1

Sometimes what you need to see may be seen first by others,
and then later by you.—S. Morrison

Now I See

$\mathscr{P}$hyllis looked down at her watch and discovered that it was 11:03 am. Her excitement intensified as each minute passed. Glancing at her watch provided evidence that time was moving mercilessly. Phyllis looked at herself in the mirror and was rendered speechless by how beautiful she looked. She felt like a princess as Tracy made final adjustments to her bustle at the Neiman Marcus Bridal Salon. She became intoxicated with joy and excitement as she gazed at her reflection.

The Christian Dior wedding gown hugged her body flawlessly. Phyllis paused and then smiled cheek to cheek. In a very soft and tender tone, she stated, "It's perfect."

Seated near the fitting room, Phyllis' mother, Mildred, and her sister, Rene, were also thunderstruck as they smiled at her. They, too, were captivated by how beautiful Phyllis looked in her wedding gown. The anticipation that filled the room was so thick that it could be cut with a knife. They were all excited because in twenty-four hours, Ms. Phyllis Sommers was going to become Mrs. Mileau Matthews. It was truly going to be a wedding that the city of Houston would never forget.

During all of the excitement, Phyllis' cell phone rang, and after the third ring, she reached into her purse, opened it, and pressed the Talk button. "Hello," Phyllis answered in a preoccupied tone.

"May I please speak with Ms. Phyllis Sommers?" A tender voice with a Southern drawl requested.

Phyllis responded, "You're speaking with her."

The voice immediately migrated to an irritated tone. "Ms. Sommers, my name is Georgia Clearwater, and I'm the assistant catering manager for the Four Seasons Hotel. I just wanted to follow up to inform you that you will have to forfeit your thirty-five-hundred-dollar deposit since you are canceling twenty-four hours before your wedding."

"I don't understand. What do you mean? I haven't canceled anything," Phyllis replied, flustered and confused.

Georgia then replied, "Ms. Sommers, I really don't have time for this. A last-minute cancellation like this is a severe disruption to our schedule because June is our busiest month. This cancellation is a devastating setback for us."

"I don't understand what you're talking about," Phyllis barked, causing her mother and Rene to stare at her.

"Your fiancé just called and said your wedding was canceled. I tried calling him back to tell him about the deposit, but your number was the only number we had on file. I have other paying clients to service. Good-bye, Ms. Sommers." Georgia then hung up.

Phyllis felt tension and anxiety rising within her. She dropped her phone. The phone rang again. She cautiously kneeled down, picked it up, and hit the Talk button, and answered, "Hello."

A sharp voice responded, "This is totally unacceptable. We manipulated our schedule just to accommodate your request."

Phyllis replied with tension in her voice, "What is unacceptable? Who is this?"

He replied, "This is Benjamin Edmonds, Ken Roomsfield's manager."

"I don't understand what you're talking about, Mr. Edmonds," Phyllis responded, feeling her heart beat faster and faster.

Benjamin then continued, "I passed on an opportunity to have Ken perform at the governor's inaugural ball." As he spoke, Phyllis envisioned entering her wedding reception and being serenaded with a violin solo as she and Mileau were officially introduced as Mr. and Mrs. Mileau Matthews.

"I just want you to know that you will lose your deposit because your fiancé canceled twenty-four hours before the wedding. What would prompt you to do something like this at the last minute?"

Phyllis' daydream was quickly crushed as she tuned back into her conversation with Benjamin. As Phyllis attempted to swallow past the knot in her throat, she felt her body initiate a silent tremble. She stated, "Mr. Edmonds, I need to call you back." She ended her call without saying good-bye. Phyllis started pacing and immediately dialed Mileau's number. She felt her head throb from the stress that conquered her. Chills covered her body.

"Hello," Mileau replied very pleasantly after answering the call on the third ring. Thoughts moved around in Phyllis' mind so fast that she couldn't concentrate on what she wanted to say first. Phyllis quickly stated, "Hey, sweetheart, there is something strange going on. The hotel and Ken Roomsfield's manager both called and said that you canceled the wedding. Is that true?" Her voice shook.

Silence covered the phone like a dark night. "I did," Mileau stated calmly after pausing a few moments.

Phyllis thought, *This isn't happening. It's only a bad dream.*

After a few moments, Mileau interrupted her thought and replied, "Baby cakes, I have a perfect explanation for you, and I would like to discuss it with you a little later. I just picked my parents up from the airport, and we've arrived at our new house. Since I don't have any privacy, I need to meet with you later, and then I can explain everything. You have my promise. I will call you later." Mileau then disconnected the call without saying good-bye.

Phyllis yelled into the phone, "No, Mileau! You need to talk to me now!" Without warning, Phyllis fainted and fell to the floor. After several minutes passed, Phyllis woke with her head in Mildred's lap, and Mildred was gently stroking the side of her face. As Mildred looked at Phyllis, she smiled as she reflected upon fond moments of how Phyllis used to lay like this as a little girl.

Phyllis stood up quickly and was terribly embarrassed when she discovered that she had fainted on the bridal salon floor. Horrible thoughts raced through her mind. She experienced a plethora of emotions that touched the unsettled shores of fear and peaked in the mountains of rage. In Phyllis' mind, things like this only happened on television—not in real life, especially not to kind and considerate people like her.

After gathering her faculties, Mildred asked her, "Phyllis, what's wrong? You were talking on the phone, and then you fainted."

As the tears began to swell in her eyes and the butterflies moved frantically in her stomach, Phyllis replied in a very low voice, "The wedding is off."

Mildred began to tremble and, with her hand covering her mouth, she said softly, "What? How could he do this to you? I don't understand."

Phyllis replied, "Neither do I. But I'm on my way to get an explanation." She stormed out of the bridal salon and then raced from the store. Mildred and Rene knew that Phyllis was on a mission, and this wasn't the time to ask questions. The rage they saw in Phyllis' eyes struck fear into them.

After getting into her Range Rover, Phyllis' mind became congested with a variety of thoughts as she blasted Jazmine Sullilvan's song entitled, "Bust Your Windows" in her CD player. It wasn't long before Phyllis pulled up at the new home she and Mileau were going to move into after their honeymoon. She approached the front door. Phyllis searched hysterically in her purse to find her key. She couldn't seem to locate it. After several frustrating minutes, Phyllis dumped the entire contents of her purse onto the ground. Suddenly, there was a loud noise. A large pink and green key chain fell to the ground with a single, silver key attached. She picked up the key with trembling hands and inserted it into the keyhole. She heard voices inside and wondered if anyone could hear her attempting to open the door.

Phyllis walked in abruptly and slammed the door. She saw Mileau's parents, along with a host of other relatives who had come into town for the wedding. She paused for a few moments as fear consumed her. Everyone looked at her but said nothing. Suddenly, Mileau's mother, Frances, and his grandmother, Louise, motioned for her to come into the dining room. As Phyllis entered the room, Frances said, "I know you are probably upset, but when you get a moment, I would like to speak with you."

"She doesn't need to speak to anyone. The only one that needs to speak to this sweet young lady is Mileau," Louise stated, her voice dripping with wisdom. The manner in which she spoke provided solid evidence that Louise was the matriarch of the family.

Oddly, Phyllis was moved when she saw her. Although they had never met, she was everything that Mileau described her to be in their past conversations. Louise was eighty-two and had white hair that was cropped and combed to perfection. She wore a pink dress and carried a matching purse that lay perfectly in her lap. Just as the pearls she wore around her neck, her graceful appearance made the wheelchair that she was bound to look like an exclusive accessory.

Louise was sitting at the dining room table, having imaginary tea in her six-year-old great-granddaughter April's tea set. Although she could not explain it, for some strange reason, the sight of Louise made Phyllis feel just a little better. This moment provided evidence of a silent connection that Phyllis was unable to articulate, nor comprehend.

Louise stated, "Hello, darling, I'm Grandmother. I've heard so much about you. It's truly a pleasure to meet you." Louise took a quick glance at the pink and green key chain that dangled in Phyllis' tightly closed hand. "Now come over here and give me a hug," she stated in a very warm and calming tone. Phyllis walked slowly toward her and bent down to hug her. As Phyllis hugged Louise, her fear climaxed. Louise whispered into Phyllis' ear, "We'll fix this soon."

Mileau entered the room from the patio door after making a few adjustments to the grill in preparation for a barbeque. He looked at Phyllis, and they stood for a few moments in silence. Louise reached for Phyllis' hand. Louise held Phyllis' hand even tighter when she realized that Phyllis was wearing white satin gloves that tenderly touched her elbows. The room was so silent that you could hear a butterfly land on a flower. "You owe me an explanation now, Mileau!" Phyllis yelled breaking the silence that dominated the room. Her rage had now consumed her. She knocked over a chair as she ran up to Mileau and stood in his face and looked directly into his eyes. Mileau could feel her breath gently stroking the hair on his mustache. Phyllis peered into his eyes with a stare so sharp and cold that it could cut steel.

April turned and inquisitively asked, "Grandmother, I thought the wedding was tomorrow. Why does she have on that wedding dress?"

Cedric, Mileau's older brother and April's father, yelled, "April, Ssshhh! Hush!"

"Cedric, please leave her alone," Louise sternly stated, as she placed her arm around April's waist and pulled her next to her wheelchair. "She is a child, and she's just asking a question—a very good question. A question that maybe Mileau has an answer to," Louise replied as she turned and looked at Mileau with a very frigid look on her face.

Although she was only six, April had enough courage to inquire about Phyllis' absurd appearance. Everyone else had not dared to mention the fact that Phyllis was in full bridal regalia. Louise turned to April and gently placed the palm of her hand under April's delicate chin and answered, "The wedding was scheduled for tomorrow. A few things may have changed, now be a sweetheart and do a favor for me. Turn your head so that I can whisper into your ear." April giggled as she anxiously turned her little ear toward her great-grandmother's mouth.

"Answer me, Mileau!" Phyllis screamed.

Mileau thought, *This all just happened too fast.* He cautiously pulled Phyllis close, wrapped his hands around her waist, and whispered into her ear, "Sweetheart, you have my promise. I will explain everything to you a little later. You know that I love you, and there is a good explanation for all of this. By the way, you look beautiful." Feeling the warmth of his hug and hearing him tell her that she was beautiful, Mileau provided her with a misguided taste of relief and an ounce of insincere hope that she was willing to accept. Phyllis understood that this moment was far greater than she. It was evident to her that she was officially in shock. She slowly pulled away. Immediately shifting the conversation, Mileau asked, "Since we have everyone here, we need to feed them. Can you take my American Express card and run to the grocery store to get a few things for a barbeque?"

Phyllis hesitantly replied, "I guess so." She put her hand on her hip and thought, *This fool is probably crazy. No, this fool is crazy! Maybe I'm crazy?* She looked him up and down.

"I've already added your name as an authorized user so you won't have any problems with using the card. I will stay here and finish getting everything else organized." Mileau stated as he handed her the credit card.

After accepting it, Phyllis exhaled a very nervous laugh and responded, "I guess I need to change." She went to her truck and pulled out a gym bag that had clothes in it from earlier that week. After changing in the bedroom, she left without a word. The topic of the wedding being canceled still remained taboo. Everyone mingled in the living room as if everything was OK.

Phyllis arrived back at the house three hours later after making an additional stop. Right before she entered the house Phyllis' cell phone rang. She answered, "Hello."

Consumed with panic, Mildred said, "This is Mother. I'm so upset! I called you over a hundred times. Rene and I drove by your apartment, but we didn't see your truck. Since we couldn't find you, we decided to go back to the hotel so that we can explain this big mess to your dad. Are you OK? Where are you? Tracy at Neiman's was going to call the police to arrest you for shoplifting. I explained to her that there was an emergency and you were frazzled and paid no attention to the fact that you ran out of the store with the wedding gown on. I paid her for the gown. It was one of the surprises that your dad and I had planned for you. Your dad is filled with rage, and I don't know what to do."

Phyllis replied, "No, Mother! This is not the way I want to handle this. Trust me. I have this situation under control. Please tell Dad that if he wants to help me, he can assist me by allowing me to deal with this matter on my own."

Phyllis suddenly felt her face tighten. She ended the call. Her mind raced to discover what she had done to deserve being treated like this. As she opened the door, Cedric saw her hands filled with bags. He grabbed the bags out of her hands and carried them to the kitchen. Phyllis quickly began preparing the food while Mileau finished preparing the grill. As she seasoned the meat, thoughts continued to race through her mind. On a conscious level, she could not grasp a reason as to why this was happening to her, but for some odd reason, she felt subconsciously that karma had come to collect a debt on an account that was definitely past due.

As she prepared the baked beans, Phyllis' mind took a journey to her past. In doing so, her thoughts quickly returned to the night she ended her relationship with James, her ex-boyfriend. It had been quite awhile since she had even thought about James. Phyllis slowly played back in her mind how impulsively their relationship had ended. Although she had dated James for three years, she had not received any indication from him as to whether marriage was a part of their immediate future. In her eyes, she had given him enough time to make a decision in regard to their future together. She had become restless.

As she peaked with dissatisfaction in regard to her relationship with James, Mileau resurfaced. Phyllis and Mileau met their freshman year at Penn State University and continued their relationship until their senior year. Since they were offered career opportunities in separate cities, fostering a relationship did not seem to have any relevance to either of them at the time. Although they had a very passionate relationship, they both concluded that their careers took more precedence than their relationship.

Seven years after graduation, Mileau ran into a mutual friend, Allison, and was able to get an update on Phyllis' life. Allison told him about Phyllis' employment and that she was not married. Acting as an informal matchmaker, Allison provided Mileau with Phyllis' contact information. Mileau hesitated to call her, but when he did, it was just like old times. Although it had been seven years, the bonds that they once shared seemed to have remained intact.

After communicating with each other over a three-month period, Mileau made a proposal to Phyllis. He explained how they had suspended their relationship to pursue their careers and now that they have both settled into their lives, he would marry her if she was willing to relocate from Detroit to Houston. Upon hearing Mileau extend his hand in marriage to her, she did not hesitate to accept his proposal.

Phyllis wanted to get married, and this was her opportunity to get exactly what she desired. Because Phyllis was employed with State Farm Insurance as a claims adjuster, transferring to Houston, Texas, was simple because of the large number of offices located there. Phyllis' plan was meticulously designed and seamlessly executed. As her plan came to a swift finish, there was one final task to complete, which was to break up with James.

Phyllis called him early on a Tuesday morning and asked if he could come over that night. As he approached her apartment, he became puzzled when he saw the empty boxes and debris sitting outside her front door. He knocked on the door. James received confirmation on his feeling that something was not quite right when she called him. Phyllis slowly opened the door. "Hello, my love. How are you?" James spoke in a very troubled tone. He tried to mask it as he attempted to kiss her on her lips. Phyllis turned her cheek to him to avoid kissing him on the lips.

He looked around, and he noticed her vacant apartment. Phyllis had packed up everything. "What's going on? Are you moving?" James stated, as sweat moved recklessly down the sides of his face and the back of his neck.

"Yes, I am," Phyllis quickly responded, as she nervously picked up the broom and began sweeping the floor. She hurried to the kitchen and placed the broom in a corner and began wrapping dishes and putting them into a box she had placed on the kitchen table.

Agitated, James repeated, "Phyllis, what's going on?"

Finally looking him in the eyes, she replied, "James, there is no easy way to say what I need to say. I guess I just need to say it. Well, I'm leaving you. After three years, our relationship has run its course, and I think it's time to move on."

James yelled, "Is this because I'm not ready to get married?"

"Yes, it is!" Phyllis yelled back.

"Well, if that's what you want, I can at least meet you halfway. Lets get engaged, and we'll set a wedding date a little later," James begged.

"No, it's too late," Phyllis said softly, as she looked over her left shoulder and thought about the items on the kitchen shelf that she had forgotten to pack.

Filled with anger, James balled his fists at his sides and took one step toward her. He focused on Phyllis' neck. James felt as though he could choke the life right out of her for causing him the pain that now consumed every inch of his body. He stopped before taking another step. As he stood motionless, James quickly came to the realization that if he overreacted and caused her any harm, he knew he would get a one-way trip, first class, to jail. Besides, he knew Phyllis was not an average woman; she probably had a backup plan that would off set any harm he attempted to impose upon her.

James quickly composed himself. "I can't believe that you're going to allow our relationship to end like this. We have three good years invested in our relationship. Phyllis, I love you. Because of that love, I want to get a few things in order with my life. I promise I will marry you."

Becoming irritated, Phyllis retorted, "I've waited long enough. The time has come for me to attain the desires of my heart. I want to get married, and I want a family. My mind is made up. Mileau, my ex-boyfriend from college, has come back into my life. Seeing as though we desire the same things, he would be an ideal husband for me. We want to get married and build a life together."

After hearing this, James felt defeated. He knew that Phyllis' mind was made up, and there was not anything he could do to change it. James concluded that it would be fruitless to continue a relationship with someone who desired to be with someone else. He was aware that he was not prepared to be the husband that Phyllis deserved and needed; James decided that he would have to accept this grim reality. Although fuming with anger, he managed to camouflage his true feelings. He grabbed her hand and held it gently as he looked into her eyes and said, "Phyllis, you're a good woman. I will always love you. I'm very sorry that it has come to this." Phyllis held back the tears she felt swelling in her eyes. James continued, "I lost, and he won. If you ever need me, you know exactly where to find me." He kissed her hand and then rushed to the door without turning back.

James loved Phyllis deeply. He just felt that he was not quite ready for marriage. He believed in being honest, and because of this, he felt he had been falsely prosecuted. However, his formal proposal without a prescribed wedding date was not enough for Phyllis. He moved too slowly in regard to giving Phyllis what she really wanted.

When Mileau proposed to her on a Monday, by Friday, Phyllis had secured a transfer to an office in Houston. By Tuesday of the next week, she had made arrangements to be packed and moved by Thursday. Her actions clearly indicated how much she wanted to get married.

As Phyllis chopped the onions to put into the baked beans, she snapped out of her journey to her past, and her reality now hit her like a ton of bricks. She was now able to see clearly that because James was not ready for marriage at that time, it did not mean that he would not be a good husband for her later. She began to take a teaspoon of ownership toward the calamity in which she had now immersed herself.

After the food was prepared, everyone gathered at the dinner table. Being a gentleman, Mileau pulled the chair back so that Phyllis could be seated. As they made preparations to bless the food, Louise stated, "Before we bless the food, I have something that I want to say to Mileau." She then looked at Phyllis and smiled. Louise continued and asked, "Mileau, can you come here for a moment?"

Mileau replied, "Yes, ma'am." He walked over to Louise.

Louise said, "You know that I love you very dearly."

Mileau nodded his head as he replied, "Yes, ma'am, I do."

Louise said, "Give me a hug." As Mileau bent down, he placed his arms delicately around her and gave her a gentle hug. As he pulled back from her embrace, "Bam!" His vision was blurred for about three seconds. He was not sure of what he saw. But he faintly remembered seeing his grandmother's purse strike his head. Blood quickly oozed from his head. Cedric grabbed napkins from the table and took Mileau to the bathroom.

Dazedly, Mileau replied, "What happened? Did Grandmother hit me?"

Frazzled, Cedric responded, "I'm not sure. We need to focus on getting you cleaned up."

"That's what you should've done, Phyllis, when you walked through that door!" Louise stated vehemently, as she gestured with her purse by pointing it in the direction of where Phyllis stood. Suddenly, a hammer fell from Louise's purse onto the dinner table.

Mildred responded, "Mother, I'm shocked at your behavior. I don't believe this. Was that necessary?"

Everyone in the room was shocked and paralyzed from what they had witnessed. Louise looked Phyllis in the eyes and stated, "My grandson clearly knows the difference between right and wrong. Young lady, I encourage you to take note. Life will present situations in which every lady has to step out of the character of that of a lady and move into that of a woman. Phyllis, sometimes you have to take drastic measures to get the attention that some situations deserve. My grandson had no right to do this to you. This wedding could've been canceled long before we all arrived here. Besides, it's cruel and devastating for any woman to find out twenty-four hours before her wedding that it has been canceled and she had no say in the matter." Mileau then walked back into the room with a bandage on his head. Looking at him with great disdain, Louise continued, "I should put another knot on the other side of your head. Maybe it will improve your thinking. Mileau, not only do you owe this young lady an apology, but also by just looking at the beautiful wedding gown she had on earlier, you owe her at least eight thousand dollars."

Phyllis searched through her emotional bank and found solace in the fact that she discovered that it could have been worse. Although it was impossible to make their situation any better, Phyllis flirted with the thought of how Mileau could have stood her up at the altar. Startled, everyone attempted to figure out where Louise had gotten a hammer. Suddenly, Cedric remembered seeing April with a hammer in her hand, but he assumed that she was taking it to Mileau when he was out on the patio working with the grill. After seeing April with a twenty-dollar bill she had been playing with, it did not take him long to figure out that April had brought the hammer to Louise.

The barbeque was ruined, but it promoted an opportunity for Phyllis and Mileau to address their situation. They left Mileau's stunned family at the dinner table and went upstairs to the master bedroom, to which they had not been granted an opportunity to sleep united under the bond of marriage. After entering the bedroom, they did not surface for two hours.

Phyllis walked downstairs, and it was apparent that she had been crying. The bandage on Mileau's head made it look as though he had been in a terrible battle. Phyllis walked over to Louise and said, "Thank you." She bent over and hugged her.

After pulling from her embrace, Louise reached in her purse. Cedric suddenly jumped up and tried to grab her purse. He yelled, "Grandmother is going crazy! She's going to hit Phyllis! Someone stop her!" Guided by her instinct, Phyllis moved in closer to Louise to prevent him from grabbing her purse.

Louise rolled her eyes and said, "I'm not going to do anything. I want to give Phyllis a little information." Louise handed her a business card. It had her phone number written on the back. Louise stated, "If you need someone to talk to, please feel free to call me."

Phyllis smiled as she accepted the card and then gently squeezed Louise's hand.

She walked to the door, paused, turned, and said softly, "Goodbye, everyone."

Mileau and Phyllis' conversation revealed how he did not think Phyllis would really jump at his offer to marry him so quickly. He also did not feel that Phyllis was really in love with him. Mileau felt that Phyllis was more in love with the idea of being married, as opposed to being in love with him. Although this was a lesson they learned together, it was truly a painful one that could have been avoided.

One month after their ordeal, Phyllis appeared in court with Mileau and was awarded fifteen thousand dollars as restitution for the loss she suffered with the wedding dress and other incidentals associated with the wedding. After the hearing, Judge Claire Alexander went into her chamber and picked up the phone and dialed. On the third ring, a voice answered, "Hello."

"The hearing just ended, my dear. It was easy for me to rule in Phyllis' favor. She will be reimbursed in full for the expenses incurred for the wedding. Oh yes, one more thing, you neglected to tell me that she bought a car with Mileau's credit card?" Judge Alexander replied.

Surprised, the voice responded, "Oh my! I didn't know that."

Judge Alexander replied, "Phyllis admitted that she purchased the car with Mileau's American Express card after leaving the grocery store to purchase food for the barbeque. She told the salesman that she would be back to pick it up, but she never returned. The full amount will be refunded back to Mileau's card without penalty. Phyllis said that she needed collateral for all of the things that she and her family had spent on this wedding. She also said that she thinks her mind just locked up on her."

The voice chimed in, "I understand what it feels like for someone to tell you they are going to marry you when they have no real intention of doing so."

Judge Alexander finished, "Is there anything else you need me to do?"

"No, that's it," the voice immediately responded. "You've done enough. My heart dropped when I saw her standing there in her wedding gown so sad and confused. Seeing her took me right back to my wedding day when my first fiancé Randall stood me up. I felt like I wanted to die. To add to this, I also noticed the pink and green key chain in her hand, which provided me with a solid indication that she was also a member of our sorority. Being a mother and a woman, I felt obligated to help her. Since I've retired from the superior court, I ran into a few difficulties attempting to help Phyllis. But when I talked to your mother, she instructed me to call you. I knew that you would take good care of Phyllis." She giggled, "I can't thank you enough."

Judge Alexander giggled and replied, "You're very welcome, Ms. Louise."

"Please send your mother my love and tell her that I will see the both of you at the alumni meeting on Saturday," Louise stated.

One year later, at 9:45 am while sitting at her desk back in Detroit, Phyllis picked up her phone and dialed a number. Approaching the fourth ring, the voice responded, "Hello."

"No, hello to you. I see you kept your phone number," Phyllis stated. Smiling from cheek to cheek, Phyllis felt nervous as she said, "Now that I'm able to hear your voice, I'm glad that you made the decision to do so. I wanted to call and apologize to you for mistreating you."

James exhaled a light chuckle and replied, "I'm OK. We don't have to discuss that. It's in the past now."

As they reacquainted themselves with a very light conversation, Phyllis shyly asked, "Do you believe in the fact that once you capture true love and it leaves, is it possible that it will return?"

James felt nervous as he replied, "To be honest, Phyllis, I really don't know. However, I'm willing to see if my true love has returned to me."

Motivation in the Moment

When you execute a plan with passive manipulation, sometimes the end result can be disastrous. In our effort to achieve some of the personal goals we desire, we can place ourselves in very complicated situations which can definitely be avoided. Although we may execute plans for selfish reasons, the productive side of this is that God has a way of utilizing a negative situation to heighten the awareness of our unhealthy behavior. From this, adversity is the learning tool that promotes growth.

During our intense moments of tribulation, a light can be ignited within you and around you. As you experience challenges, you may be placed in a position where only a specific situation can provide you with the growth that can only be achieved from that perspective. To add to this, as we encounter challenges, there is a voice inside that sometimes warns us of danger. We have to be open to listen and respond accordingly. When we are not aligned with it, we sometimes ignore it and suffer grueling realities.

In some instances, we are blind to the fact that we may be in need of assistance. Amazingly, God has angels who are earthly bound who masquerade as everyday people to guide and assist us. Through the ignition of the light within each of us, combined with the light of our earthly bound angels, we are graciously guided back to our purpose on the path of righteousness.

The Awakening

Please respond accordingly.

Question #1
Can you think of a situation in which you have utilized passive manipulation to get a result that you desired?

_____

_____

_____

_____

Question #2
Was the end result to your advantage or disadvantage?

_____

_____

_____

_____

Question #3
What did you learn?

_____

_____

_____

_____

CHAPTER 2

Avoiding the responsibility of accepting reality for what it really is can place you in very challenging circumstances. —S. Morrison

The Comfort Zone of Denial

"Excuse me, Noble, I really hate to bother you, but there is a police officer in the lobby requesting to speak with you immediately," Aretha, Noble's assistant, stated as she abruptly entered his office. Becoming infected with her nervous energy, Noble quickly laid the paperwork that he held in his hand on his desk and headed for the lobby.

When he entered the lobby, he saw the police officer standing with his back turned, looking out the revolving glass door. The police officer turned around when he heard Noble enter the room. Noble said, "Hey, Milton. What's up?"

Feeling somewhat relieved as he greeted his friend, Milton smiled and exhaled a nervous chuckle. Milton made a deliberate attempt to compose himself as he approached Noble and whispered into his ear, "I'm sorry to bother you like this, but I have a little situation that warrants your serious attention. Can you step outside with me for a moment?"

Noble felt nausea climbing within him. His mind became overwhelmed with outlandish thoughts as he wondered what Milton wanted to tell him that was so confidential. As they exited the building, they walked toward the police car. While walking, Milton stated, "I was dispatched to attend to a call this morning from one of the Target stores requesting assistance in regard to a shoplifter."

When they finally arrived at the police car, Noble's jaw dropped when he saw his mother, Ella, sitting in the front seat of the car. Noble was perplexed and stunned. His mind was now devastated as he unsuccessfully rummaged for an answer as to why his mother, at the age of seventy-three, was caught shoplifting. When Noble's eyes met his mother's, all he could see was a vision of the sweet and kind lady that made the best chocolate chip cookies that he had ever tasted.

Ella was forty-one when Noble was born. Because of the enormous age difference between Noble and his siblings, he lived a life like that of an only child. He was definitely showered with an enormous amount of love and affection from both of his parents. Because Ella was his only living parent now, he felt obligated to attend to her every need. Before opening the car door, Milton stated, "This is really difficult for me to bring this situation to you because Ms. Ella has always been a wonderful person to me. I can vividly remember as a kid how I practically lived at your house. We ate the best chocolate chip cookies after softball practice when we played in the little league." Milton smiled as he laughed nervously. He quickly continued, "Because of that, I didn't have the heart to take her down to the police station, but I needed to do something. That's why I brought her here to you. I think there is something serious going on with her."

Noble quickly opened the door. As calmly as he could, Noble stated, "Good morning, Mother. How are you?"

"I'm fine," Ella replied irritably.

Noble continued, "Mother, Milton says that you are under the suspicion of shoplifting. Is that true?"

She quickly and defensively stated, "No, it isn't! I went there to buy a pair of socks to match my outfit. Listen, Noble, I'm the parent, and you are the child. I don't have to answer to you." While Noble was standing in the opened area of the car door, Ella reached for the handle of the car door and attempted to close it.

She yelled, "Move!" Embarrassed, Noble stood there speechless as he moved out of the way and allowed her to close the car door.

Noble noticed that his mother was wearing a very short, navy blue pleated skirt that had a thick baby blue pinstripe at the bottom of the skirt. She also had on a matching navy blue top that had the initials T.H.E. embroidered in white.

Milton placed his arm on Noble's shoulder and stated, "Please don't feel ashamed. I'll take care of everything. I just wanted you to be aware of what's going on. I'll be glad to take her home for you." At that moment, Noble knew that would probably be the only and best thing to do. Puzzled, Noble stood there scratching his head.

He looked at Milton and stated, "I can't thank you enough. Again, I will definitely talk to her when I get home. Meanwhile, I will speak with my brother and sister and make them aware of what has happened."

Milton smiled and said, "Don't worry. I'll take good care of Ms. Ella. You know she's like a second mom to me. I will call you after I get her settled." Noble nodded in compliance.

As they pulled off, Noble attempted to search within himself to discover an answer. He began rubbing the back of his neck as an attempt to pacify the tension he felt climbing within him. Noble knew something needed to be done, but he had no idea what his next move would be. After arriving back at his desk, he decided to call his oldest brother, Ryan. Now totally bewildered, he picked up the phone and dialed Ryan's cell phone number. On the first ring, he answered, "Bank of America, this is Ryan."

"It's me, Noble," he stated, with the intent of aborting Ryan's greeting. "I know that you're probably very busy. However, I wanted to call and tell you that we need to do something about Mother. We have a problem."

"What do you mean?" Ryan stated sharply.

"She was almost arrested for shoplifting this morning. If it wasn't for my friend Milton, she would probably be in jail. Thank God, he was the officer that was dispatched to attend to the call." Noble humbly offered.

"Listen, Noble. I'm very busy. I'm working on a very high profile project, and I really can't be bothered with disruptions like this. You live with Mother; the least you can do is keep a good eye on her."

Noble replied, "Thanks for your help, Big Brother." Noble's frustration climbed higher. Feeling defeated, Noble slammed the phone down onto the receiver. He was not bothered by the fact that he disconnected the call without saying good-bye to Ryan.

The more he thought about their mother, the more Noble became irritated over Ryan's lack of concern for her. Noble's anger climbed even higher as he reflected upon the fact that Ella was responsible for securing Ryan's job at Bank of America. Ella had a solid contact who was the director of human resources, who also happened to be a very dear friend of hers. Therefore, getting Ryan hired was an easy task.

Noble's mind then settled on thoughts of his sister. He picked up the phone again and dialed. On the third ring, a pleasant voice answered, "Abbott Laboratories, this is Marthony."

"Hey, sis. How are you?" Noble asked.

"I'm well," Marthony stated, providing evidence that she was definitely in a good mood. Just hearing her voice seemed to make him feel relieved.

Noble quickly replied, "Marthony, we have a problem." Silence intercepted their conversation. Noble continued, "My friend Milton just picked Mother up for shoplifting."

"Shoplifting? I don't believe it!" Marthony stated, now infected with irritation.

Noble quickly responded, "She was caught shoplifting in Target, and my friend Milton just happened to be the police officer dispatched to the call. Because of him, Mother was not arrested."

"I don't believe it. There has to be more to this story. She's an elderly woman, and they don't do things like that. Furthermore, I refuse to continue to listen and engage in a conversation that assassinates the character of our mother," Marthony stated attackingly.

Taking a defensive stance, Noble stated, "Guess what Mother had on when she was picked up?"

"What did she have on?" Marthony replied nonchalantly.

Rhythmically, Noble stated, "Mother had on a pleated skirt that had a thick baby blue pinstripe at the bottom. She also had on a matching navy blue top that had the initials T.H.E. embroidered in white."

"OK. She had on a T-shirt and a skirt. So what? I can't see where this conversation is going," Marthony replied sharply.

"Does that ring a bell?" Noble stated sarcastically.

Marthony quickly responded, "No, it doesn't."

Fuming with anger, he replied, "Well, allow me to assist you in unlocking the mystery, Marthony. T.H.E. stands for Township High East. She had your old high school cheerleading uniform on. Now, explain that!" Noble slammed the phone down onto the receiver disengaging their call.

After terminating their call, Noble searched intensely to gain an understanding as to why his brother and sister reacted in the manner in which they did in regard to their mother. He was stumped by the fact that his brother, who was twenty-two years older than him, and his sister, who was twenty years older, offered absolutely no assistance with the problem that had been recklessly placed before them. Because they were both established in life, Noble felt that they would both be a solid resource in dealing with this matter. At this point, Noble came to an immediate realization that they officially exonerated themselves of any responsibility toward attending to this situation and any other that surfaced regarding their mother. To his dismay, not only was he left disappointed, but he also felt abandoned.

Noble could not shake the feeling of helplessness that consumed him. The wonderful, caring mother that had taught him not to lie, cheat, or steal had now become an active participant in the things she adamantly spoke against. Noble had returned home to live because he was in the process of purchasing a home for himself. He felt that living at home would prove to be beneficial to him and his mother. In doing so, it was an automatic assumption by Ryan and Marthony that Noble would assume all of the responsibility toward attending to this matter and any other situation pertaining to their mother.

In the two years that he had lived at home, Ryan and Marthony were never exposed to the other occurrences that involved Ella. After informing Marthony about their mother's shoplifting incident, he knew that it would be impossible for her to believe how Ella misbehaved in the grocery store.

While shopping, an elderly woman took Ella's basket by mistake. After discovering that her basket was taken, Ella initiated her silent witch hunt for the culprit. Upon locating her basket, Ella, consumed with rage, pushed the woman into the Frosted Flakes cereal display and caused it to tumble down upon her. After taking her basket back and in the absence of witnesses, Ella was not held accountable for her actions.

Noble only became privy to this occurrence because Ella threatened to do the same to him when he was under suspicion for stealing money from her purse. To add to this, Noble definitely could not forget the time when he was at the bank with Ella. As they prepared to depart the bank, the bank teller approached Ella, grabbed her hand, and placed something into her hand and closed it. She stated, "Place that somewhere safe." She gave Ella a hug. After hugging her, she rolled her eyes at Noble and walked off. When they got into the car, Ella opened up her hand and discovered that the young lady had given her twenty dollars.

Ella later told Noble that she had informed the bank teller, whom she had known for several years, that she was not being fed and that she was being physically abused and neglected. Ella was not bothered when she informed Noble of the lie she told. Feeling embarrassed, Noble now understood why the bank teller had rolled her eyes at him.

As his mind wandered back to the present, Noble felt that he had indirectly victimized Milton by engaging him in his personal issues. When he arrived home that evening, his conversation with Ella revealed that she did not recall what had transpired that morning. In fact, she refused to have any dialogue with him in regard to her shoplifting.

The following Thursday, Milton called Noble and said, "I have something that I think you need to hear."

Inquisitively, Noble replied, "What is it?"

Milton stated, "Well, I think it's best that I just let you hear it." Milton clicked over to the next line in order to activate his three-way calling. He then dialed and accessed his voice mail. Noble heard the introduction to the voice mail state, "Thursday, October 26, 10:20 am."

Noble's heart fluttered as he heard, "Hello, Milton. This is Ms. Ella. I've been thinking. First of all, you don't have to call me Ms. Ella anymore. You can just call me Ella. You're an adult now. I have to admit that it was truly a pleasure to be escorted home by you last week. I think you have grown into a strong and courageous man. I now realize that you are no longer the little boy that used to play with Noble. You're a man now—an extremely handsome one if I have to say so myself and a man that I'm deeply attracted to. I know this may come as a shock to you, but I owe it to myself and to you to honor my feelings. Since my husband died eleven years ago, I haven't thought about another man. But there is something about you that I find alluring. I know this may cause you to feel a little odd because of your ties with my son. But guess what? It really doesn't matter whether Noble knows or not. In fact, I don't care if you tell him about this message. I'm an adult, and I can date whomever I desire.

Please give me a call on my cell phone when you receive this. The number is 706-555-1212. I'm looking forward to hearing from you, my love. Good-bye."

As the message ended, Noble remained silent. He tried to collect his thoughts to say something. The first thing he could mutter was, "I apologize, Milton. I guess she retrieved your number out of my cell phone when I left it in the kitchen."

As he exhaled a very heavy chuckle, Milton stated, "It's no problem. I think it's funny and wild. It's nice to know that your mother thinks that I'm attractive and she wants me to be your new daddy." Noble laughed with him as he pretended not to be bothered by what he had just heard.

Noble knew something needed to be done. He knew that he had to begin to search deep within himself. Although he was ready to move into a new home of his own, with so many things going on with Ella, his conscience would not allow him to execute his plan. Noble felt that if he left Ella alone something dreadful would happen to her.

He then reflected on the Friday afternoon while frying fish, Ella had decided to take a nap, only to be woken by a fireman, as he rescued her from her bed in the smoke-filled house. This event coupled with fact that Ella occasionally wandered off in the middle of night caused Noble's mind to reside in a state of frenzy. Remaining committed to taking care of his mother, Noble animated himself to any situation that Ella presented to him.

Several years passed before he could successfully discourage Ella from leaving in the middle of the night. Noble was able to prevent her from leaving because he slept in a sleeping bag in front of her bedroom door. In doing this, Noble eventually found himself completely exhausted.

After constant encouragement from Milton, Noble finally took Ella to the doctor. She was officially diagnosed with dementia. Upon receiving this news, initially, Noble felt abandoned and isolated again. Suddenly, his sentiment changed. He discovered that it had already become routine to be his mother's caregiver. Although he had siblings, life presented him with a situation where he was forced to attend to his mother by himself.

After sailing in the troubled waters of denial, he docked on the shores of acceptance in regard to this grim reality. Through the acceptance of the reality that his mother was ill, he began taking the first step in the right direction. Noble had already endured sleepless nights and immeasurable amounts of stress. He quickly realized that the obstacles that he had already endured had provided him with a protective armor. As he came to understand dementia and it serving as a possible precursor for Alzheimer's disease, he devoted himself to Ella. Indeed, he found it truly difficult to comprehend the fact that someday when her health diminished beyond the realms of receiving care from him, he would have to surrender and allow professional care to be provided.

Slowly Noble found solace in the fact that he would rather endure the struggles of being his mother's sole caregiver. Surrendering Ella's care to anyone else was an option he refused to take. Noble understood that when a person does not have all of their faculties, very few people will take the time to become a caregiver. He knew that his life had officially been placed on hold. Serving as a caregiver was a contract that God ordered on his life only to be fulfilled by him.

Motivation in the Moment

When hardships occur in the family unit, those who we think will serve in the capacity of support sometimes falter and offer no support. When this occurs, it definitely provides an opportunity for the actions of others to be highlighted for better or worse.

Those who cannot and will not provide assistance in attending to the care of a loved one will become easily recognized. In addition to this, certain circumstances can provide an opportunity for those who are willing and able to rise to the occasion to gingerly maneuver closer to God by functioning as a caregiver in the spirit of service. It is through compassion and humility that they are granted an opportunity to magnify the presence of God in us as spiritual beings.

As a society, we are capable of dealing with diseases and a variety of illnesses, but when it comes to matters of the mind such as dementia, Alzheimer's disease, or any mind-altering disease that disarms a person's mental capacity, some become cold and turn away. Often, when this transpires, the burden is shifted to a select few or a specific person that is willing to carry the title of being a caregiver.

Indeed, this is a difficult position to assume under any circumstance. However, the beauty in this is that God has already blessed the caregivers. He blesses the caregivers by providing them with an opportunity to be a blessing to someone else.

The Awakening

Please respond accordingly.

Question #1
Can you think of a situation in which you were in denial?

_____

_____

_____

_____

Question #2
Why do you think you were in denial?

_____

_____

_____

_____

Question #3
How did you come to terms with your situation? If not, what steps are you taking to come to terms with your situation?

_____

_____

_____

_____

CHAPTER 3

*Although some may never speak of the facts,
it doesn't mean they are not aware.*—*S. Morrison*

Tacit Secret

"Tiffany, we're going to be late. Let's go!" Carlton yelled from the driver's side of the car. She scrambled through the items in her purse as she attempted to find her key to lock her front door. After madly blowing his car horn, Carlton yelled loudly, "If we're late, we're going to miss the opening ceremonies, and it's going to be your fault!" Tiffany found her key, inserted it into the keyhole, and locked the door.

Concentrating on each step she took, Tiffany moved as quickly as she could in her stiletto heels. When she arrived at the car, she opened the passenger door and carefully got in. She smiled vibrantly, which was a clear display of her admiration of how handsome Carlton looked in his black suit, accented with a crimson and cream tie.

Just the sight of him made her feel special. Carlton was everything she needed at this time in her life. Carlton turned to Tiffany and said, "After all of these years, you still haven't changed. I thought once we left high school you would've improved. Then I thought maybe by the time we finished college at NYU, you would've seized a hold of it, but that didn't happen. Then I figured maybe after you began your career, you would've grabbed a hold of it. Sadly, after seven years of serving as the director of finance for St. Clair County, I thought you would've grasped a hold of your time management and improved your punctuality." He smirked as Tiffany pulled a bottle of Gucci perfume from her purse and sprayed it on her wrists and then rubbed them together. Tiffany maintained her silence as she crossed her leg and closed the car door.

Tiffany turned to Carlton and calmly replied jovially, "I'm responsible for managing money, not time. Now let's attend to the matter at hand. Driver, you may now leave." Tiffany laughed insanely, causing Carlton to become infected with laughter. She leaned over and gave him a gentle kiss on the cheek.

Because Tiffany and Carlton's ties as friends ran half their life span, they were truly the best of friends. After a short introduction from Tiffany's older sister, Margaret, while they were both freshmen in high school, a great friendship had blossomed.

Tonight, they were on their way to a reception which was being held in Tiffany's honor in recognition of her outstanding performance in managing the city's budget. It was an event that they both were looking forward to attending. Due to their very busy personal and professional lives, it was truly an opportunity for them to reconnect and catch up on the current events in each of their lives for that week.

Shortly after they arrived, the ceremony began, and Tiffany was presented with her award. Carlton beamed with pride as Tiffany commanded the attention of everyone through her appearance and the assertive tone of her voice. When she finished her acceptance speech, she returned to her table. While sitting there, Carlton smiled and looked Tiffany in the eyes and stated, "I'm so proud of you." He hugged her and kissed her on the cheek. Carlton then placed his hand on her knee and rubbed it tenderly. Tiffany smiled as the waiter approached the table and noticed Carlton's hand on her knee. Carlton quickly made their meal selection and returned his attention to Tiffany. He then stated, "Your speech was truly remarkable. But when I think about it, I'm not surprised. You have always been brilliant." He smiled and placed his hand on her back and gently rubbed it in a circular motion. Tiffany giggled.

Their public displays of affection often caused them to be easily mistaken for a couple. Truly, it did not matter to them, since shortly after they met, they officially adopted each other as brother and sister. Their ties were misunderstood by many, but their relationship was strictly platonic. In their eyes, the love they held for each other was far greater under the bonds of friendship. Their platonic love possessed an elegant mystique that only Margaret really understood.

As the evening progressed, Carlton looked at Tiffany again and stated, "Your eyes are a little red. Are you feeling OK?" She quickly grabbed her purse and retrieved her compact mirror. She looked and discovered that Carlton was correct in his scrupulous assessment.

Tiffany replied, "I'm just a little tired, that's all. I'll be fine after a night of good rest." Tiffany smiled and began picking at the grilled chicken on the plate in front of her.

Shortly after dinner, they left, and Carlton dropped off Tiffany at home. As she prepared to get out of the car, she looked him directly in the eyes and said, "Thanks for an awesome time. Give me a call to let me know that you arrived home safely."

Carlton quickly responded, "I sure will." She kissed him on the cheek. He reached over and gave her a very robust hug. Tiffany got out of the car and went into the house.

After entering the front door, she kicked off the stilettos that now caused her feet to ache. She headed directly to the bathroom. When she turned on the bright lights and looked into the mirror, she noticed that her eyes had turned a darker shade of red. As Tiffany grabbed the washcloth that lay on the towel rack and ran cold water on it, her mind immediately migrated to the conversation she had earlier with Carlton regarding her eyes. It was then she remembered she had made a deliberate decision not to take her medication.

On this day, she just wanted to be free to celebrate the recognition she had received from the city. Tiffany was being honored, and she possessed a desire to just feel normal. She did not want to be committed to taking the medication she was required to take daily. Carlton had a tendency to go into emotional overdrive when she got sick, so she dared not tell him about her awful decision. Tiffany knew if she did, he would have placed the entire evening on hold just to go back home to retrieve her medication.

Tiffany began to experience her flu-like symptoms, which were initiated with nausea and achiness. She noticed that sweat had started cascading down the sides of her face and that her hair had become very damp. Suddenly, a vomiting spell seized control over her. It was so intense that it caused her to pull a muscle in her chest. At this point, she knew that she had gone too long without taking her medication and that now she would need medical attention. At this moment, Tiffany discreetly accepted and regretted her poor decision.

After her third vomiting spell, the phone rang. She felt that it was almost impossible for her to answer it, but if it was Carlton, she knew that she needed to tell him so that he could come to help her. Tiffany looked at the number that appeared on the caller ID and saw the number 618-555-1212. It was Carlton. She felt an ounce of relief to her tenuous body that was now aching all over. She slowly reached for the phone and in a raspy voice answered, "Hel-lo."

"I made it home," Carlton stated. There was a short pause in their conversation. Carlton said, "Did you hear me, Tiffany?" Silence monopolized their conversation once again. He asked, "Is everything OK?"

After wiping her mouth with the washcloth that she held tightly in her hand, she responded, "No, it's not. I think I need to go to the emergency room."

"I'm on my way!" Carlton shouted, quickly ending their call.

Thirty minutes passed, and then there was a loud knock at the door. Tiffany tried to muster enough strength to get to the door, but she took so long that Carlton decided to open it with his spare key. As he entered the bedroom, he saw Tiffany lying conscious but motionless, on the floor. When she saw him, she grinned and said, "Please don't be mad at me. I just couldn't take all of that medicine today. This day was too special for me."

"Tiffany, being mad at you is the last thing on my mind." Carlton smiled as he kneeled down and picked her up. He stated, "We need to get you to the hospital." He carried her to the car and drove her to the hospital.

Upon arriving at Southside Hospital, Carlton pulled up to the emergency entrance and carried Tiffany inside. Once inside, the emergency staff placed Tiffany in a wheelchair and took her into the emergency room. Meanwhile, Carlton provided the admissions nurse with details on the evening that led them there.

After providing all of the necessary information to admit Tiffany, Carlton sat in the waiting area thirty minutes. During his short wait, he could not come to grips with the thought of leaving Tiffany alone. He went back to the nurses' station and talked to the nurse sitting at the desk. "I'm here with Tiffany Whittington. My name is Carlton Whittington. I'm her brother, and I think she's going to need me." He stated authoritatively.

The nurse looked at the sheet of paper attached to the clipboard and stated, "She's in room four." She hit a buzzer granting Carlton entrance to the secured area of the emergency room.

Carlton always made it a point to tell the staff that he was her brother in order to gain entrance to the treatment area. Several years earlier, when he accompanied Tiffany to the emergency room, he was denied entry because he was not an immediate family member. Since then, stating that he was her brother was a little secret lie they had agreed to tell for him to gain access to her whenever she was in the treatment area.

When Carlton walked into her room, he saw Tiffany lying helplessly on the hospital bed. Seeing her in the formfitting black dress that she wore earlier caused his heart to race. He immediately sat down and listened to the doctor and nurses begin their ritualistic probe. Carlton grabbed Tiffany's hand and looked her in the eyes and stated, "She has AIDS, doctor. She fell behind in taking her prescribed cocktails today."

The doctor then asked Tiffany, "How long have you been infected with AIDS, Tiffany?" She replied, "About ten years." The doctor responded, "Let's go ahead and get an IV started to keep her from becoming dehydrated."

Carlton reached over and grabbed a tissue from the box next to her bed and began wiping sweat from Tiffany's face. As he gently wiped her face, Tiffany smiled and weakly said, "Please don't mess up my makeup." They both smiled, which eased Carlton's pain. This moment provided another opportunity to strengthen the bonds of their friendship.

As he smiled, he calmly replied, "I promise I will not disturb your million-dollar-MAC makeup job."

His smile made Tiffany feel a little more at ease. He had become a master at attending to her every need when she experienced a crisis. Since her sophomore year of college, Carlton was the only person Tiffany felt comfortable enough with to make privy to her illness. He vowed to never tell anyone and remained her sound source of support.

Although he eagerly assisted her, during episodes like this, he often wondered how Tiffany's family would react if they knew how sick she was. Taking a different approach, Carlton questioned, "Tiffany, maybe you should tell your parents what's going on with you?" Tiffany motioned her head left to right to indicate no.

Lifting her head slowly, she replied in a raspy and clammy voice, "They would never understand. I've thought about telling them, but I think they may treat me differently. If it weren't for the fact that we grew up in Dustin, Alabama, I would. I just don't think they're ready. They wouldn't understand an illness like this."

He quickly decided to change the subject and focus on making her comfortable. After a few hours, they were able to stabilize her. She was kept overnight for observation but was released early the next morning.

Carlton dropped her off the next morning, and she went into the house, sat down in the living room, and thought about the impact of possibly dying without granting her family an opportunity to assist her. Carlton's concern about telling her family about her illness ran through her mind over and over. Finally, she came to the conclusion that she would tell Margaret about her long battle.

As the sun's glare penetrated the room, Tiffany reached into her purse for her cell phone. She sent a text message which read, *Please call me ASAP*. Several minutes later, her phone rang. When Margaret's name appeared on her caller ID, Tiffany answered mellifluously, "Hi, Margaret."

"What's up?" Margaret inquired. Tiffany crossed her legs and thought about how sick she really was. She looked down at the red flats that Carlton had put on her feet to take her to the hospital. Tiffany began shaking her foot, and her shoe dangled from her big toe.

She replied, "Margaret, I want to tell you something, but I hope that you won't treat me differently after I tell you."

Tiffany got nervous, and Margaret replied, "OK. I promise I won't."

Tiffany said, "When I was at NYU, I contracted HIV. Shortly after I graduated, it progressed into AIDS. I've been dealing with this for about ten years by myself. Well, let me clarify that. Carlton and I have been dealing with my illness for a long while. Because we didn't use protection, I contracted it from a boyfriend that I had at the time. I discovered that I had it in a very odd manner. One day, after Carlton and I returned to the dormitory after our economics class, I entered the lobby and was immediately stopped by my resident assistant, a police officer, and a member of the board of health.

"They had come to arrest me because my ex-boyfriend Jacob, with whom I had severed ties four months earlier, had listed me as one of his sexual partners during an interview he had with the health department after being diagnosed. It was their assumption that he had informed me and that I hadn't come in to seek medical attention. They thought I had chosen to deliberately infect anyone with whom I had engaged in a sexual relationship. As mandated by law, this action would be considered a felony. A person is contagious in their HIV and AIDS status, and it is then considered a lethal weapon, due to the fact that it is a fatal disease that can kill. They had come to incarcerate me to prevent me from infecting others.

I immediately explained to them that he never told me that he had AIDS. When I heard this, I felt as though I had been slammed into a brick wall. I thought, 'AIDS? HIV? Me? Infected?' I instantaneously broke down into a deep sob and fell to the ground. Because of my reaction, they knew I was telling the truth. The police officer immediately escorted me to the health department, where I had my blood work drawn. I not only discovered that I had contracted AIDS, but that I also had syphilis and that it had been feeding on my organs. Through all of this, I had not received any indication from my body that I was ill. I knew that I had contracted the virus from Jacob because he was the only person with whom I had ever been sexually active.

Sadly, he died shortly after we finished college. I didn't say anything because of the negative stereotypes that surround this illness. During this experience, I felt like I was all alone. At the time, Carlton was the only person that I felt would understand, so I confided in him. I just couldn't confide in anyone and believe that they would understand my situation. I felt that I had landed myself in this situation, and I thought it was my responsibility to navigate through it.

Last night, I got severely ill, and Carlton took me to the hospital. While there, he told me I needed to tell someone besides him."

Margaret sat silently as she listened to every word Tiffany spoke. Tiffany heard sniffling, which served as an indication that Margaret was moved by her confession. She seemed to understand why she and her parents were excluded from Tiffany's silent struggle.

Margaret replied, "When I came to visit you about two years ago, I was putting on my makeup, and I went under your sink to get a cotton swab. I saw your medicine bottles sitting in a basket, and I couldn't help but notice your prescriptions. When I read the prescriptions, I knew exactly what they were for. They were drugs administered only to AIDS patients. I've become familiar with these drugs because my friend Edward has been battling AIDS for about three years. During his struggle, he has enlightened me on the numerous drugs he takes for treatment. I will admit that I was terrified. I knew if you hadn't told me that it wasn't my place to question you in regard to your health. Tiffany, there were many occasions when I wanted to say something, but I was just too afraid. I understand that you are an adult, and I didn't want to offend you and isolate you from us. I've always felt uneasy about the possibility of you needing us and being helpless. At least now I can help you. You're my sister, and I don't mind. That's my job as a big sister. Just because I never said anything, didn't mean that I didn't know. I'm truly thankful that Carlton has been there for you, and I want you to know that I love you and that I'm here for you as well." Tiffany smiled as her fears of rejection melted and migrated to the shores of hope and liberation.

Motivation in the Moment

When an illness strikes, it can cause those we love to respond in a variety of ways. Some may even resort to extroverted and introverted behaviors. The cause and answers to these behaviors exist only within each person.

Often we become exposed to situations that are far beyond our realm of understanding. As we encounter these incidents, it is best to provide each person with an intense level of respect for their privacy in regard to their health. The best way to aid a person in such a situation is to allow them to see your actions, which should be anchored in love. Allow the silence that they maintain to be your understanding until a desire is ignited within them and they desire to make you privy to their struggle. Truly, we can deny those we love the right to evolve as spiritual beings through exclusion. This manifests itself by aborting their growth opportunity by prescribing actions under the opinion that others will never understand.

Although you may have opinions before a situation unfolds before you, concrete opinions can be adjusted. Once you are in a situation in which you are coerced to taste, breathe, smell and, most of all, exist in, a transformation in one's thought process can easily occur. The reality of the situation will salute you and those involved sooner or later. Nonetheless, if a reality exists where there is a presence of unpleasant circumstances, indeed it is truly up to each individual to decide if they want to move forward. Whether you accept it or not, the answer resides only within you.

The Awakening

Please respond accordingly.

Question #1

How do you respond when you are asked to keep secrets?

_____

_____

_____

_____

Question #2

When you became privy to the secret, what challenges did you face?

_____

_____

_____

_____

Question #3

What was your final outcome? If you are still engaged with a particular situation, what steps are you taking to come to terms with your situation?

_____

_____

_____

_____

CHAPTER 4

*When obstacles surface, those whom you may least
expect will come to your aid.—S. Morrison*

Facing the Unexpected

"*I* made it!" Sarah thought as she bolted out of the elevator and headed to her office. It was 8:31 am, and she was exactly one minute late. This Monday morning was just as difficult as any other morning. After arriving, Sarah placed her attaché case in the chair in front of her desk.

Sarah felt a little relieved because she had successfully made it through another morning filled with a variety of challenges as she made preparations to begin her and Leilani's day. After experiencing a few moments of ease, without warning a very uneasy feeling quickly surfaced within Sarah. While taking off her coat, the phone rang. "MGM Studios, this is Sarah Howell," she stated pleasantly.

"Hello, Ms. Howell. This is Ms. Key, one of the staff members here at Kindercare. I know that you just dropped your daughter Leilani off about thirty minutes ago, but she just had a seizure. We've called the paramedics." Ms. Key stated with in a worried tone.

"I'm on my way!" Sarah shouted, as she immediately dropped the phone and grabbed her purse. The tension that now consumed her caused her to feel as though her heart was beating so fast that it would explode at any moment. Sarah had only enough time to stick a Post-it note on her computer in an attempt to notify anyone that came by her office of her family emergency.

The day care was a twenty-five minute drive from her job. Sarah was oblivious to the fact that she made it there in thirteen minutes. After arriving in a flustered state, Sarah was informed that Leilani had been stabilized. Because this was the first time she had a seizure, Sarah was advised by the paramedics to take her to the emergency room. In fear of Leilani's condition taking a sharp turn for the worse, Sarah openly accepted their recommendation and allowed the paramedics to take Leilani to the hospital. While riding in the ambulance, Sarah, although frightened, understood that she needed to be strong for Leilani. Sarah did everything she could to mask her anxiety. As the paramedics conducted their initial assessment of Leilani, Sarah held her hand tightly. She constantly repeated to

Leilani, "Everything is going to be fine." Strangely, each time she stated that to Leilani, Sarah realized that it provided her with more comfort for herself than it did for Leilani. After arriving at the hospital and completing a plethora of tests, things seemed to move very rapidly. Sarah suddenly realized that it was 11:30 pm and that an entire day had marched briskly by.

The test results concluded that Leilani had suffered a seizure due to a kidney infection which could be resolved by taking antibiotics. Shortly after receiving this update, Leilani was discharged and was granted approval by her doctor to return to school. The next day before entering the day care, Sarah kneeled down to get eye level with Leilani and said, "Mommy loves you very much." As Leilani held Snuggles, her favorite stuffed teddy bear in her right hand, Sarah placed her arms around Leilani's little waist and gave her a very robust hug. "Mommy really wishes she could stay a little while longer with you, but Mommy has to go to work so that she can pay our bills. Things will get better, Leilani, I promise," Sarah stated as tears collected in her eyes. Feeling choked up, Sarah continued, "Remember, you are Mommy's big four-year-old. Mommy needs you to be a very big girl. Because you're such a big girl, I need you to help Mommy. Your Uncle Ethan is going to pick you up from school today. You're going to stay with him and your Aunt Cherie until I can come and pick you up later tonight. I need you to promise Mommy that if you start to feel sick, you will tell Ms. Key so that she can call Mommy and I will come and pick you up."

Leilani smiled and quickly replied, "OK, Mommy." Sarah extended her hand to Leilani, and she gently placed her hand in Sarah's as she stood up. Sarah held Leilani's hand tightly as they entered the day care.

Once inside, Sarah approached Ms. Key. She gave her a hug for being so responsive and taking good care of Leilani. While speaking to Ms. Key, Sarah felt a small tug on her coat pocket. She then saw Leilani proceed toward the play area. Sarah watched her closely. Sarah was moved as she admired Leilani in the little navy blue dress complemented by her meticulously combed hair, accented with gold barrettes. Leilani stood as the epitome of her relentless love. Sarah felt that the longer she stayed, the harder it would become for her to leave.

Sarah had become sullen and discouraged because she was attempting to become the best mother she could be to Leilani. However, due to the pressing demands of being a career woman and a single mother, she had to come to terms with her situation by attending to her responsibilities not only as a caregiver but also as the sole provider of their family unit. Because of this, Sarah knew she had to return to work immediately. In addition, if she was going to send Leilani to a good college and provide her with a solid start in life, she had to save and invest wisely. Because of this, the reality of returning to work did not remain a total discomfort to her.

After arriving back at work, Sarah noticed that her anxiety continued to climb. When she walked into her office, she prepared to take her coat off. Before pulling it off, she reached into her pocket. Suddenly, Sarah's mood changed. She smiled when she discovered that tug she had felt while speaking with Ms. Key was when Leilani had placed Snuggles in her pocket. Looking at the weathered, beautiful, brown teddy bear, wearing a baby blue bow tie, reminded Sarah of how much comfort he brought to Leilani and why she loved him so much.

Sarah opened the bottom drawer of her desk and gently placed Snuggles on top of the paperwork in the drawer. Throughout the day, she could look down at Snuggles and be reminded of her precious Leilani. Because she longed to be with Leilani, Sarah decided that she would spend her lunch break at the day care. Meanwhile, she uploaded a picture of Leilani to her cell phone and saved it as a screen saver. In doing so, for each call she answered, she would see Leilani's warm and tender smile, which provided her with the momentum to make it through the day.

When Sarah pulled up her e-mail, she discovered that she had received fifty new messages in her inbox. Among them was a message marked urgent, which was sent to her from Chris Kerrington, her manager, requesting to see her immediately. After reading the e-mail, Sarah darted off to his office. She entered his office with a smile that only she knew had been deliberately and painstakingly placed on her face and stated, "Good morning, Chris. I received your message. You need to see me?"

Sitting behind his desk in the very quiet and scrupulously decorated office, he glanced at his watch and then responded, "Yes, I do. I need the marketing proposal that you are working on by tomorrow."

As Sarah's voice trembled, she stated, "I don't understand. The date that we agreed to submit the proposal was exactly one week from today."

Emotionlessly, Chris replied, "Correct. Things have changed. It's due tomorrow. Oh yes, when I walked by your office at 8:30 am yesterday, I noticed that you were not here on time. In addition to that, you left for the entire day without being excused. It will be mandatory that you make up those hours immediately."

Apologetically, Sarah stated, "I'm very sorry. My little girl was very ill, and I had to take her to the hospital. I had already planned to work late today to make up the lost time."

Sternly, Chris stated, "Please make sure that you do that. I hope you are aware that what you did can be considered as abuse of company time. To add to this, you can be terminated for your actions. Although your daughter may be ill, it doesn't mean that our daily operations have to cease. You have a responsibility to this company, and I expect you to attend to it accordingly. I dismissed the last person in your position because she had a father who was very ill, and it caused her to be absent excessively. Because I felt she was a liability to the company, I decided to terminate her. I'll overlook it this time. This is a story that I don't hesitate to share because it's up to you whether or not you would like to be added to this story line as well."

As Sarah prepared to exit his office, she took three deep breaths. She began a silent prayer in her mind, "God, please give me the strength to withstand this obstacle that has been placed on my path. I may not understand the things that are going on around me, but I'm aware that if you have brought me to my current station in life, you will bring me through this."

Purposely changing the topic of their conversation and interrupting her silent prayer, and while sniffing obviously, Chris questioned, "What's the name of the perfume you are wearing? It smells very sweet and pleasant."

Staying focused, Sarah quickly responded, "Thank you. I really want to make sure that everything is perfect. Is it possible for us to focus on the original date that we negotiated?"

Chris got up from behind his desk and stated very calmly, "I don't think that will be a good idea." He walked around his desk and approached Sarah. Chris then looked Sarah directly in her eyes. "We need to stay a few steps ahead of our competition. Because of that, we need to work a little longer, harder, and smarter," he stated, as he placed his hands near her shoulders and began massaging her arms gently. Chris continued, "If you need me to help you, I'll be more than happy to stay after hours and assist you." Providing a cynical smile, he stated, "That's what good managers do. They help their subordinates who are loyal and willing to go the extra mile for the team." He then gently swiped his index finger under her chin.

Sarah stood there motionless. Her emotions went haywire. She became extremely nervous, and then her mood migrated to anger. She tried to convince herself that it was all in her mind. However, Sarah's budding desire to punch Chris in the face made her realize that this was really happening. She maintained her composure as best as she could. She took one step back and barked loudly, "No! I don't need any help. I will take care of it myself." She then quickly exited his office.

Filled with nervousness, Sarah went into the restroom in an attempt to compose herself. Sarah paced back and forth so hard she felt as though she was beginning to grind groves into the floor. After staying in the restroom about thirty minutes, Sarah went back to her office. She knew that she had to attend to this matter. As she analyzed her situation, she was left with no choice but to quickly tap into her inner self to find enough energy to make it through the long day and night that lay ahead.

While working diligently, Sarah looked up at her clock and discovered that it was 7:11 pm. Everyone had gone home, and only she and the members of the cleaning crew remained in the building. Due to the anxiety associated with completing the proposal, she did not have much of an appetite and moved through the entire day without eating. Now feeling thirsty, Sarah went to the break room to get a soda. She felt that the caffeine would give her the necessary boost to make it through the rest of the night.

After a very short break, Sarah returned to her desk and continued working on the proposal. She sat with her back facing the entrance of her office. Sarah glanced at her clock again, and it was 9:34 pm. Maintaining her focus, she resumed her work on the final portion of the proposal that would probably take another two hours to complete. Nonetheless, she began to feel a little relieved because she felt the end was coming soon.

While keying information into her laptop, Sarah felt something warm on her right breast. She looked down and discovered it was a hand. With her back still turned, she pushed her chair back and screamed, "Get off me! Help!" The movement of the chair caused the wheel on the chair to roll and pinch his toe. As he bent over to grab it, Sarah picked up the stapler and whirled it around and hit him in the head. Because his hands were positioned to absorb the blows that were intended for his head, Sarah was oblivious as to whom her attacker was.

As Sarah prepared to swing again, his hand moved exposing his face. Sarah replied, "Oh, my God. It's you!" He replied, "I'm sorry. I didn't mean to catch you off guard. I told you that I would come in to help you."

Consumed with rage, Sarah yelled, "I don't want or need anything from you, Chris!"

Attempting to compose himself, Chris barked, "Yes, you do! You need your job."

Sarah stated, "Let's see." She reached for her cell phone. Chris attempted to grab the cell phone from her, and it fell on the ground.

"I know that you're not going to call the police."

Sarah screamed, "Get your hands off of me!"

"Are you OK, Sarah?" A very deep and authoritative voice questioned.

Totally frazzled, Chris turned around and saw Sean, a member of the evening cleaning crew. Forcefully, Sean inquired, "Is everything OK?" Chris released both of Sarah's wrists which he had held tightly.

He then looked at Sarah and stated, "I'll see you in my office in the morning." Chris knew that it was in his best interest to now walk away. Because Sean was about six foot five and weighed about two hundred and fifty pounds, Chris knew that he would be no match for him.

Sarah began packing up her belongings in preparation to make an immediate departure. After picking up her cell phone off the floor, Sean handed it to Sarah. He observed how intensely Sarah's hand was trembling as she took the phone. Sean asked, "Are you OK, Sarah? If you don't mind, I would prefer to walk you to your car."

Sarah quickly nodded her head and said, "I would really appreciate it. Thanks."

Once she arrived at her car, Sean handed Sarah a piece of paper with a phone number written on it. He stated, "If you need anything, please feel free to call me." Still frazzled, Sarah accepted the piece of paper and opened her car door and quickly got in. Because Sarah worked after hours so frequently, Sarah had become familiar with Sean when he came in to clean the office at the end of each day. After a few conversations during her coffee breaks while Sean cleaned the break room, it was not long before they exchanged war stories on the struggles of being good parents and developed a bond of friendship.

After starting her car, Sarah lowered the window and said, "Thank you very much. I don't know what I would've done without you, Sean. I can't thank you enough."

Sean smiled and replied, "He will not bother you again."

"I can't thank you enough for helping me," Sarah stated again as she drove off. As she drove, Sarah gripped the steering wheel so strongly that she felt as though she could bend it with her bare hands. Sean's presence had prevented Sarah's situation from getting worse.

Fueled with rage, Sarah knew that she needed to develop and initiate a plan of action. However, she was clueless as to what the first step would be. In her quest to discover an answer, she concluded that she needed to file sexual harassment charges against Chris with the human resources department immediately.

The following day at the moment she arrived in her office, Sarah's phone rang. On the first ring, she answered, "MGM Studios, this is Sarah."

"Good morning, Sarah. I need to meet with you and Chris immediately. You both can come to my office," Sharon, Chris' immediate supervisor, stated.

"Yes, I'm on my way," Sarah replied as she held the phone tightly. Sarah's mind raced in an attempt to discover what was going on.

When Sarah entered Sharon's office, her heart began to beat so hard that she felt as though it was going to come through her blouse. Sarah wrestled violently with herself to maintain her composure when she observed Chris' narcissistic smirk on his face. His comfortable and composed demeanor provided solid evidence to Sarah that she was not the first person that he pushed himself on. Sarah knew that she had to maintain her composure even though her mental state was in total disarray.

Sarah painted another vivid mental picture in her mind of punching Chris in the mouth, which brought a very warm and tingly sensation through her entire body. Sarah said, "Good morning. How are you this morning, Sharon?"

"Not too well," Sharon replied blandly.

Inquisitively, Sarah stated, "Is there a problem?"

Sharon sharply replied, "Yes, I have a problem with your punctuality. Also, Chris has brought it to my attention that you took it upon yourself to excuse yourself during company hours to attend to a personal matter."

Suddenly, Sarah thought, *What nerve. He didn't say that when I stayed until 11 o'clock in the evening for the last five weeks, working on the last project I was assigned.*

Authoritatively, Sharon replied, "This is the second time in the last eight months that you have been tardy. Your workday begins at 8:30 am, and it ends at 5:00 pm. I find this to be totally unacceptable." Sarah searched desperately to discover why she was being singled out and treated like this. In another attempt to maintain her composure, she relished the thought of punching both of them in the head with her bare fist.

Sarah maintained her composure and replied, "Sharon, please accept my apology for my tardiness. I know that it's unacceptable, and I will not allow it to happen again. Yesterday, my little girl fell ill shortly after I dropped her off at day care, and I had to rush her to the hospital."

"Personal issues are to be resolved during your personal time and not during company time. You leave me no choice but to suspend you while we conduct an investigation which will determine whether or not we will terminate you. Chris will be in contact with you in regard to the results of our investigation. Please surrender your company badge," Sharon stated emotionlessly as she extended her hand.

"What? I can't believe this," Sarah replied. In an attempt not to make matters worse, Sarah slowly removed the badge that was attached to her blouse and placed it gently in Sharon's hand.

Clasping the badge in her hand, Sharon stated, "You are dismissed. Thank you for your time."

Sarah walked out of the office. As she headed back to her office, she felt defeated. Sarah walked into the restroom and closed the stall. She started to cry. Sara muffled her moans with the tissue that she held balled up tightly in her hand. She knew that if Chris and Sharon saw her in this state, they would only use it against her.

After about twenty minutes, Sarah went back to her office to collect her coat and purse. She continued to make a deliberate effort not to display how emotionally worn she was. Sarah then thought of Leilani. She decided that she would make good of the situation and spend the rest of the day with Leilani. The thought of being able to go and spend the day with Leilani provided Sarah with some relief for her aching spirit.

The moment she walked back into her office, the phone rang. Sarah pondered whether or not she would answer it—especially now, since she was officially suspended. She thought of Leilani and how the call could be about something regarding her. Sarah quickly grabbed the phone and said, "MGM Studios, this is Sarah."

"Sarah Howell?" The voiced stated very warmly.

"Yes, this is she," Sarah responded.

"Hi, I'm Vanessa Hemming from the human resources department, and I've been assigned to assist you in regard to the assault that occurred with you and your manager. On the behalf of the company, I would like to extend our sincerest apology. We want you to know that we are here to assist you in any way that we can," Vanessa stated.

After hearing this, Sarah's heart dropped. It provided her with some relief, but she began trembling. Sarah's mind raced to discover how Vanessa became privy to what had happened.

Vanessa continued, "The director of human resources, Maurice Thomas, has called an emergency meeting with you, Chris, and Sharon. We really need to speak with you now. When Mr. Thomas arrived at his office this morning, he discovered a photo of you and Chris that had been circulated around this department."

"I don't understand what you are saying. What do you mean there is a photo of me and Chris circulating around?" Sarah barked furiously into the phone. Sarah hoped she was asleep and engaged in a bad dream that she would awake from very soon. With anger and frustration swelling inside, Sarah wondered what she had done to create the chaos that had now surfaced before her.

Sarah felt like the whole world was crumbling right before her. Vanessa continued, "It is a photo of him holding your wrists in a very aggressive manner. It definitely looks as though you were being attacked. There were copies taped on the walls in the hallway that leads to the entrance of the human resources department, on the door to Mr. Thomas' office, on his assistant's computer, and a stack of copies were left on top of the copy machine."

"Yes, I'm available," Sarah quickly replied. "Let's go. I have a lot I need to say."

Compassionately, Vanessa stated, "I'm on my way up to your office right now. Please wait for me, and I will escort you into the meeting."

Sarah replied, "I will do just that. Thanks." After ending the call with Vanessa, Sarah exhaled the breath that she had been holding in for awhile. She thought about how wonderful God is.

When Sarah entered the office escorted by Vanessa, she noticed that Chris' narcissistic smirk had turned to that of an expression of worry that was written all over his face. The presence of Mr. Thomas caused Sarah to smile inside as she glanced at one of the copies that lay gingerly upon the desk in front of Chris. The facts orchestrated an undeniable case of how Chris abused his authority as Sarah's manager. A sexual advance made toward a subordinate is not an acceptable behavior for a member of management under any corporate umbrella. Sarah realized through this encounter that her true strength had been with her and that it lay within her. By maintaining her composure, she was capable of dismantling a plan that had been strategically assembled to destroy her.

While sitting in the meeting, Sarah searched within her mind to discover who had taken the picture and had posted copies in the human resources department. Sarah reflected on the words, "He will not bother you again." Just as the words danced around in her mind, she looked up and saw Sean walk by the office door pushing a trash cart. It was unusual for him to be there in the morning. As Sean passed by the partially opened door of the office, he positioned himself so that Sarah would notice him. Without locking eyes with her, he looked down and removed his cell phone from the carrying case attached to his waist. He pretended to be reading a text message. After about five seconds, he looked up and saw Sarah looking at him.

Sarah received the answer that she was seeking. As she put the pieces together in her mind, Sarah discovered that Sean was the only person who was there and who would have access to the building to post the photos in the manner that they were displayed. Sarah winked her eye at Sean. He quickly placed the phone that he had used to take the photo back into its carrying case. Sean then discreetly pushed the trash cart away from the entrance of the door. Sarah crossed her leg and sat back comfortably in the chair as she witnessed justice being served to her workplace aggressor.

Motivation in the Moment

We are often placed in circumstances in which we are forced to deal with adversity in a manner which we do not find comfortable. As responsible spiritual beings, we are encouraged to always look at the bigger picture and place our faith in God. He truly has the solution. Although we may find it complicated to understand the solution, yet we must remember that God holds the blueprint to our lives. Because of obligations which support our livelihood, we are forced to move quickly through adversity. In turn, this is a blessing in disguise.

This is due to the fact that before our mind is granted an opportunity to concentrate on the problem, we are forced into circumstances which are bound in a solution. The solution is moving forward. When we allow ourselves to act as opposed to reacting, we grant ourselves an opportunity to move strategically through obstacles. In addition, sometimes simple encounters can lead to very strong and intense bonds of friendship, formally and informally. A cool mind can conquer anything and it is truly the light in the midst of darkness.

The Awakening

Please respond accordingly.

Question #1

Describe an instance in which you were forced to deal with a situation that was beyond you.

_____

_____

_____

_____

Question #2

How important is it to you to maintain your composure when dealing with adversity?

_____

_____

_____

_____

Question #3

Describe a situation in which you lost your composure. Was the impact positive or negative?

_____

_____

_____

CHAPTER 5

Sometimes we are oblivious as to who is watching us.
Be prepared when it's played back to you. —S. Morrison

Lasting Impressions

"Carmen! Did you hear what I said?" Jason screamed as he pushed her into the wall. He pushed her so hard that her elbow punctured a hole in the wall. He then pinned her against the wall. Carmen trembled as she looked into his eyes and felt the pulse of the burning rage he no longer held captive. This episode was not like the others. This time she knew he was consumed with anger. Carmen nodded her head in compliance in the hope that he would release her. Jason grabbed her by her throat and looked her in the eyes again and stated, "You are not going to leave me. The only way you're going to leave me and your kids will be in a casket. If you would like me to, I can definitely arrange that."

Carmen could not believe this was happening again. Three years earlier on Christmas Eve, Jason broke her finger when he was angry with her about the house not being clean enough. She made a silent promise that she would leave Jason the next time he hit her. After seven years and several fractured bones, Carmen discovered that she had lost count of the next time. Although Carmen felt that Jason was a horrible husband, he was an excellent father to their son and daughter.

As the years passed, the relationship that Carmen had adored so much had become one that she regretted and hated. The man that she once loved tenderly had become her greatest aggressor. This was a painful reality for Carmen because she felt alone. She knew that everyone would be shocked if they were exposed to the darkness in their bond of marriage.

Carmen refused to tell anyone because Jason created an image of being a perfect father and husband whenever he was in the presence of others. Carmen felt that it would be impossible to convince anyone to believe the years of physical and mental abuse she had endured. The only friend that knew her dark secret was Gregory. After meeting and working in the same beauty salon with him for over seven years, they had developed extremely close ties as friends.

The next day when Carmen entered the salon for work, her hair was frazzled, and she did not have her normal polished appearance. Gregory smiled as he usually did when he saw Carmen walk through the door. When she arrived at her work station which was next to his, Gregory said, "Good afternoon." He extended his cheek to her, which served as her cue to place a soft and fragile kiss on it. He smiled and asked, "How are you?"

Carmen smiled hesitantly and replied, "I'm OK."

Gregory quickly focused on the large bandage that was on her elbow. After discovering it, his face tightened. He approached her and whispered, "He's at it again?" Carmen placed her purse on the shelf next to the sink and grabbed her smock. As she tied the smock around her waist, Carmen tried to think of something to tell Gregory so that he would not worry. However, they had become so in tune with each other emotionally as friends that he was perceptive enough to tell whether or not she was telling the truth.

Hesitantly, she replied, "Yes."

Gregory felt tension climbing within him. He looked at Carmen and said, "Carmen, why do you allow Jason to beat you like that? He can only do to you what you allow him to do."

Feeling discouraged, she replied, "We had a little disagreement, and now it's resolved. Things like this happen from time to time. When I was a little girl, I remember my mother and father having problems, too. This is normal. That's what men do when they get mad. Right?"

Gregory reached over and took Carmen gently by the hand and said, "Come with me." He then walked her to the receptionist's desk and told the receptionist, "Carmen and I are going to run a quick errand. I have something I need to give her. Tell my next appointment and Carmen's first appointment that we will be back in a few minutes."

Without resistance, Gregory walked Carmen to the door and held it open for her. After leaving the salon, Gregory took Carmen's arm and wrapped it in his. They walked to his truck which was parked in a very secluded area of the parking lot. Gregory leaned against his truck and said, "I'm worried about you, Carmen."

Carmen quickly responded, "I'm fine, Gregory. I'll get through this like I always do."

Gregory quickly interjected, "That's the problem. You are always trying to make it through. I'm afraid that one day you may not. Carmen, a real man doesn't exert his authority by beating on a woman. I can't tell you how to manage your life, but I can tell you that as a friend, I'm worried about you being in an abusive relationship. Do you think this is how a respectable man treats a woman? I want you to think about how I've treated you. I'm a man. But have I ever mistreated you?"

Carmen was now forced to reflect on the countless times Gregory had held the door open for her and how he had always been nothing but a gentleman. Carmen focused on the numerous times that he had treated her to lunch and how Gregory relentlessly complemented her on her inner and outer beauty.

Truly, it was no surprise to her why Gregory's appointment schedule was always booked. Gregory treated every lady that he encountered with the highest level of respect. He made all of his clients feel special. In addition to this, Gregory made Carmen feel that she was special just by the tender manner in which he spoke to her.

"Carmen, I've known you for seven years. You were the first person to befriend me when I was hired at the salon. Over the years, I've watch you evolve from being a top-notch stylist, to becoming a bride, who became a terrific mother, who has evolved into a battered spouse." Carmen stood facing Gregory with her arms folded as she listened attentively but remained motionless while looking into the distance over her left shoulder. Carmen wanted to collapse in his arms because she knew deep inside everything that Gregory stated to her was true.

In a defeated tone of voice, Carmen replied, "I really want to leave but now is not a good time. I don't want my children to grow up without a father. I think it would be too devastating for them if I were to divorce Jason."

"I disagree," Gregory quickly responded.

Taking an inquisitive stance as to why he responded in the manner that he did, with a perplexed look on her face, Carmen asked, "Why do you disagree?"

Gregory continued, "I disagree because I think overcoming the devastation of their father killing their mother is a far greater grueling reality than overcoming their divorce. Well, that's all I have to say on that. Now, I'm feeling a little hungry. Let's go to Applebee's for lunch, and it's my treat."

Thrown by the quick change of subject, Carmen hesitantly responded, "That sounds great. I'll drive."

Time passed quickly, and it wasn't long before they returned from lunch. Gregory made up his mind that he would not badger Carmen. Because he loved and cared for Carmen, he decided that he would support her in spite of any decision she made in regard to her dysfunctional marriage.

At the close of the day, Carmen prepared to go home. Before she walked out the door, Gregory shouted, "Carmen! Wait up. I need to tell you something." He walked briskly toward her, opened the door and allowed her to walk through it. Once outside, Gregory stated, "Carmen, you're my friend. I love you, and if you or the kids need me, please call me." He hugged Carmen and quickly released her and went back into the salon.

After leaving the salon, Carmen went to pick up Iris and Jeffry from school. When Carmen pulled up closer to the curb, she noticed that the principal, Mr. Morgan, was standing with Iris and Jeffry. After parking the car, Iris and Jeffry ran to the car to get in. Mr. Morgan walked to the driver's side of the car and said, "Hello, Mrs. Parker. I'm Mr. Morgan the principal here at Sumnter Elementary. I have a very urgent matter to discuss with you regarding Jeffry. If you don't mind, I would like to have a word with you. Could you please come with me to my office?" Feeling uneasy, Carmen turned her head and looked at Jeffry as he sat in the backseat quietly with his head down. Because Jeffry had been a well-behaved student, this was truly out of the norm for him to be in trouble with the principal.

Mr. Morgan continued, "It's OK to park your car here. Mr. Thorpe, the crossing guard, will be glad to stand outside the car with the kids and wait for you to return." Carmen replied, "OK." She got out of the car and followed Mr. Morgan into his office.

After they arrived in Mr. Morgan's office, Carmen anxiously waited to see what warranted such an impromptu parent conference. After sitting down, Carmen took note of the awards Sumnter Elementary had received for being such an outstanding school. Carmen smiled, feeling an ounce of relief. This reaffirmed her decision to send Iris and Jeffry there. Carmen truly wanted the best education for her children, and she knew that Sumnter Elementary would definitely provide it.

Mr. Morgan closed the door to his office. He then sat in a chair next to Carmen. He stated, "Mrs. Parker, I need to speak with you because of what transpired with Jeffry and another young lady in his class. It has been brought to my attention that Jeffry refers to Myra as his girlfriend. I do understand that it's normal for children at the age of eleven to pair up and mimic adult relationships. However, this morning during recess Jeffry had Myra pinned up against the wall and stated to her, 'You are not going to leave me. The only way you're going to leave me and your kids will be in a casket. If you would like me to, I can definitely arrange that.' Because Jeffry made a threat on her life, we have to take this matter seriously." When Carmen heard this, she felt a cold rush coupled with fear consume her. She felt embarrassed because part of her secret had been exposed in an honest, but inappropriate manner. Carmen rummaged through her mind to discover how Jeffry heard the argument between her and Jason. Carmen became perplexed as she tried to calculate how many times Jeffry and Iris heard Jason attacking her. Suddenly, Carmen felt an unexplainable shift inside. Her body was there, but her mind had departed.

When Carmen's attention returned to the conversation, she heard Mr. Morgan say, "Mrs. Cranford stated that Jeffry is her top student and that she has never had problems with him. She pleaded with me not to suspend him. She asked if I would speak with you and bring it to your attention so that you can attend to this matter accordingly." Carmen held the strap of her purse tightly. She crossed her legs and maintained a composed face and carefully constructed a response in her mind.

Carmen responded, "I apologize, Mr. Morgan. I can assure you that this won't happen again. In my son's defense, I have an idea of where he heard that statement. He probably heard that from something he watched on television. Nonetheless, I'm going to speak with him immediately. Please tell Mrs. Cranford that I apologize and that I extend my sincerest thanks to her for being so understanding."

Carmen shook Mr. Morgan's hand and quickly departed. Reciting the lie that she knew she had to tell caused a light inside Carmen to ignite. When she got back into her car, she remained silent. As she drove home, silence monopolized the mood in the car. After arriving home, Carmen parked the car in the garage. Jeffry and Iris got out and entered the house. Following close behind them as she entered the kitchen, Carmen said, "I need to speak to the two of you." Jeffry paused first because he knew he was in trouble.

Iris turned around and looked at Carmen and stated, "About what, Mommy? Jeffry got into trouble today, not me."

Iris and Jeffry sat down at the breakfast table. Carmen sat down facing them. Softly, she stated, "Jeffry, I owe you an apology. I'm sorry that you heard me and your dad arguing in our bedroom. What he said to me wasn't very nice, and it's not an acceptable way to speak to anyone. What you said to Myra today was inappropriate. It was very mean and rude." She turned her head and looked at Iris. She smiled as she looked at Iris and saw a reflection of herself. Softly, Carmen said, "I owe you an apology, darling. I've allowed myself to be disrespected and mistreated as a lady. If a man loves and respects you, he won't hit on you. I'm sorry because I feel like I haven't been a strong role model for you. It's my job to teach you how to be a lady. I've set a bad example for you, and now I have a mess that I need to clean up. In doing so, I'm going to leave your father. I want you to understand that your dad and I love you both dearly. However, as good parents, it's our duty to provide you with a safe and happy home. Right now, we don't have that, and I need to make that happen immediately. I know this is a shock, but we are going to leave right now. I want you to go to your rooms and start packing your things. I will be in there to help you in a few minutes."

Regret consumed Carmen as she packed their clothes. She could not think about anything else but leaving. In thirty minutes, she packed enough clothes for her and the kids to last the next couple of days. While loading their bags in the car, Iris handed Carmen her pink suitcase and stated, "I'm not mad at you, Mommy. You don't have to be sorry." She hugged Carmen.

Jeffry then hugged Carmen around her waist and said, "I'm sorry, Mom. I'm glad we're leaving. Iris cries herself to sleep when you and Dad argue, and I'm tired of sleeping on her floor." Carmen felt her heart drop as she hugged Iris and Jeffry with each arm. The warmth in their affection provided a solid indication that she was headed in the right direction.

Jason arrived home that evening and discovered a note that Carmen left indicating that she and the kids had left. Jason was very upset and called Carmen on her cell phone in an attempt to reconcile. He pleaded, cried, and promised that he would never hit Carmen again. However, Carmen remained committed to her decision to leave. The expense of having ties to a public gentleman and a private assailant had become a bill that she could no longer satisfy.

It took a year to finalize their divorce. During that time, Carmen moved in with her parents and saved enough money to purchase a home for her and the kids. Healing was a long journey, but it was a journey that Carmen truly welcomed. The strong support system that she developed among a few friends had remained in tact, especially with Gregory.

As time passed and she was able to put her divorce behind her, Carmen discovered life was definitely complicated, but not unbearable. On a normal day at work and in between clients, Gregory and Carmen sat in the break area to talk. Carmen felt a little hungry and rose from the table to purchase a candy bar from the vending machine. Gregory grinned as she glared at the limited selection. When she turned around she asked, "What are you smiling about?"

Gregory quickly responded, "I'm grinning about you."

"What do you mean about me?" She stated coyly. After sitting next to him, Gregory pulled her chair even closer. Still puzzled, Carmen remained silent.

Gregory stated, "I'm so happy to see where you are now. I can look at you and see how good life has been for you. It's unfortunate that things didn't work out for the better between you and Jason." As he spoke, Carmen's eyes remained focused on the Pay Day candy bar that she had begun to play with. Gregory said, "It's truly his loss. I'm so relieved now. I need to tell you something."

Looking puzzled, Carmen replied, "I'm listening."

Gregory continued, "When Jason hurt your elbow, I tossed and turned the whole night. I never told you this, but I was very angry. I thought about attacking him on several occasions. Each time I prepared to do so, I realized that I was overstepping my boundary as your friend. I didn't want to face the risk of you becoming angry with me and possibly losing your friendship." He smiled and grabbed Carmen's hand and questioned, "Do you know what I discovered that night as I lay in bed tossing and turning?"

Carmen replied softly, "What?"

Holding her hand and looking in her eyes, he replied, "I discovered that I was in love with you." Carmen became very nervous. Although she felt a little uneasy, she admitted that she, too, had developed a fondness toward Gregory after her divorce. She had dismissed her feelings as a mere desire for companionship. Reality presented her with the fact that her friend now stood before her as a perfect gentleman. Gregory continued, "I know that you're probably shocked, but this is how I feel. I discovered that I can't control who I love and fall in love with. Being a true man, I'm willing to speak up and go after what I desire, and what I desire is you."

Carmen felt chills consume her body. The feelings that surfaced made her realize that it had been awhile since a man had spoken to her in such a warm manner. Carmen replied, "What would become of our friendship?"

Still gazing into her eyes, Gregory responded, "Our friendship is everything."

Carmen smiled and shyly stated, "What do you mean?"

Gregory stated, "Friendship that is anchored in love will last a lifetime."

Motivation in the Moment

When physical abuse enters a relationship, the relationship has taken a devastating turn for the worst. Not only do those who are victims of the abuse suffer, but also those that surround them. People can only harm you if you grant them permission to do so. Permission is often granted in the form of remaining present in a relationship that involves physical, mental, and emotional abuse.

Although it may be extremely difficult to remove yourself from the equation, it is important to remember that God placed us here to love and be loved in return. Whenever you are in the presence of someone and your prescribed definition of love involves pain, it is not true love. It is only a poorly developed replica of love. True love has an ability to surface in many different forms.

Friendship as a precursor to love is a magnificent opportunity to partake in a relationship that has a solid foundation. The respect that friendship provides will grant love an opportunity to blossom beyond the imaginable.

The Awakening

Please respond accordingly.

Question #1
Describe a situation in which you felt that you were mistreated.

_____

_____

_____

_____

Question #2
How did you attend to it, or what steps are you now taking to attend to it?

_____

_____

_____

_____

Question #3
If you neglect to attend to it, what impact will it have on you?

_____

_____

_____

_____

CHAPTER 6

When opportunities for advancement are met with rejection,
remember to salute rejection with resilience.—*S. Morrison*

Down but Not Out

"Xavier, believe me. I hate to do this, but this situation is really beyond me." Alexander stated compassionately.

Xavier sat in the chair with tension pronounced in every muscle in his face. "I do believe there is something that you can do. I've been here for thirty-one years. Doesn't that mean anything?" Xavier responded.

"Yes, it does mean a lot. But we have to cut back, and your department has been outsourced to India," Alexander stated, maintaining a calm demeanor.

"I can't believe this. I think you have forgotten, Alexander, the fact that you didn't have any experience when you were hired. I took a huge risk when I hired you. Now that you have been promoted ahead of me, you are now going to lay me off," Xavier stated as he stood up.

Still sitting behind his desk, Alexander replied, "I haven't forgotten, and that's why you were the very last person left working here in my department. I've done everything in my power to keep you here. The reality still rests in the fact that effective Monday morning, this department will officially cease operations here in the United States. Trust me, Xavier. If I could do something, I would do it."

As Xavier listened and acknowledged the sincerity in Alexander's voice, Xavier replied, "You're right. I know that you've done everything in your power to help me keep my job. I'm just irritated over what lies ahead in regard to my future."

Alexander stated, "If you take the retirement package being offered, you will leave with something. Meanwhile, you can live off of your retirement and look for another job."

Irritably, Xavier stated, "I'm fifty-nine. Who would want to hire me?"

Alexander quickly responded, "Companies and organizations are looking for seasoned leaders. Xavier, I want you to prepare a detailed résumé to expose your talent for leadership. This is what I'll do for you. I'm going to refer you to a good friend who writes résumés, and

I will pay for it. Please list me as a reference, and I will provide you with a good letter of recommendation. I know things may seem a little complicated, but I think you have more to offer than what you realize."

Although still consumed with fear, Xavier found relief in the assistance Alexander wanted to provide. He stated, "Maybe you are right. I guess maybe my skill sets may be more profitable in an alternative arena."

Alexander gave him a business card for the résumé writing service he had mentioned earlier. Xavier said, "I apologize for the things I said. I was just upset, and it was wrong of me to take my frustrations out on you."

Alexander smiled and responded, "Apology accepted. Just promise me that you will call me if there is anything else that I can do to assist you." Xavier smiled, and then a security guard entered the office to escort him off the premises.

Although it was company protocol in a situation like his, Xavier was still a little upset over the fact that he was not granted an opportunity to pack up his own office. Xavier was escorted by security out of the building to his car. He was told that his personal items would be delivered to him by FedEx the very next morning.

On the next morning, the box with all of his personal items from his office was delivered to his door. Reality quickly settled in. Xavier knew the time to act on his future had come. He contacted Alexander's friend, submitted his information, and had a professional résumé prepared. Several months after posting his résumé to Web sites such as careerbuilder.com and monster.com, he received an e-mail from Kaiser Permanente requesting an interview. After responding, a date and time for an interview were set.

When the date arrived, Xavier felt a little nervous, but he knew that he had a lot to offer. Xavier was confident as he successfully moved through the preliminary rituals of the introduction with Sally, the hiring manager.

Sally commented, "How long were you at the last company you worked for?" Xavier replied, "I was there for thirty-one years. I was preparing to celebrate my thirty-second year with the company before I was forced into retirement."

Surprised, Sally stated, "Wow! And you still want to work?"

Xavier placed a plastic smile on his face and continued to enlighten Sally about his colorful background in regard to his work experience. Upon completion of the interview, Xavier felt that he had given Sally his best, but he did not feel that would be enough. He knew that time would tell everything. Several weeks passed before he received confirmation in the form of an e-mail which stated that she found a more suitable candidate. Although he was disappointed, he discovered that his inner voice was correct. The comment which Sally made about Xavier's tenure at his last job made him feel a little uneasy. Although subtle, it seemed that Sally was not very receptive to hiring an older yet seasoned candidate.

Xavier refused to be bothered. After living as long as he had, life had presented a plethora of experiences in which he had no choice but to master resilience. On the following Wednesday, he was invited to attend another interview. Upon completion of that interview, he had discovered once again that subtle references regarding his age had begun to surface.

Because Xavier was good at saving money, he could maintain his standard of living for several years. Xavier had already paid off the mortgage on his home. This eliminated a huge expense which reduced the pinch of being unemployed. After six months of being unemployed, Xavier felt defeat growing stronger inside of himself. Xavier was frustrated, but he was open to accepting any job that would give him a chance.

On an early Tuesday morning at 7:30 am, Xavier's phone rang. He answered, "Hello."

"Good morning, Dad. How are you?" Preston said.

"I'm fine, Preston. It's good to hear your voice," Xavier responded.

"Dad, I have a problem, and I hope that you can assist me," Preston stated.

Without hesitation, Xavier asked, "Are you OK, son?"

Preston replied, "I feel uncomfortable asking you this. But you know I wouldn't ask you for a favor if I really didn't need help."

Becoming a little irritated, Xavier stated, "Son, what is it?"

"We have run into a few problems with staffing at my store. The person that I hired to perform the custodial duties quit without any notice. I will have a replacement in about three weeks. Meanwhile, I need help. I never thought owning a Smoothie King would be this hard. It is impossible for me to do everything by myself."

Xavier exhaled a very light chuckle and stated, "Well, son, I'm not doing anything else."

"I'll pay you for your time, Dad." Preston eagerly offered.

"No, son," Xavier quickly replied. "It's an honor and a pleasure to be available to assist you. It's my job as a good father to help you, especially when you are trying to help yourself."

Preston laughed and said, "Thanks, Dad. I can't thank you enough."

"What time would you like me to come in?" Xavier asked.

Preston responded, "If you can be here in an hour that would be great."

"I'm all yours," Xavier replied eagerly.

"Thanks again," Preston said before hanging up the phone.

Although working as a custodian was indeed a major career shift, but if it meant that it would be a benefit to Preston, Xavier would welcome this new employment opportunity. It would also grant him an opportunity to redirect his focus onto something else other than being unemployed.

Several weeks passed and Preston received confirmation of what a big help Xavier had been to him. He wore the title of being a custodian for his son proudly. Not only did he clean the store well, but he was also instrumental in reorganizing and managing the inventory. Xavier functioned as his son's most prized asset which was evident in Preston receiving a perfect score on his most recent health inspection.

The next day Xavier arrived for work at 8:30 am and walked into the inventory room. After hearing him enter, Preston said, "Dad, can I speak with you for a moment?" Preston led him into his office. After entering the office, Xavier immediately sat down. Preston grabbed a chair and moved it next to him.

With a puzzled look on his face, Xavier stated, "Is there something wrong, son?"

Preston smiled and replied, "No, Dad, there's nothing wrong. I just wanted to tell you how thankful I am to have a dad like you. But I just don't understand why you still refuse to accept money from me."

Xavier smiled and responded, "You're my son, and I love you. I want to do everything in my power as a good parent to ensure your success."

Preston smiled, placed his hand on Xavier's leg, and stated, "I have a proposition for you. I know that you want to go back to work, and I think I can help. Because you have been such an asset to me with getting this location running well again, I would like to hire you as an operations manager. You will be responsible for this location and the new location that I've decided to open. Business has done so well that I'm prepared to offer you a very attractive compensation package. I have to pay someone, so I would rather pay you."

Xavier was speechless. This was too much for him to handle. He had difficulties processing all that he had heard. The little boy that he had taught how to play baseball and ride his bicycle stood before him now as a prospective employer. Xavier looked at Preston and smiled. He said, "A good father should always be willing to help his son. I was so focused on being good to you that it never crossed my mind that the young man I eagerly desired to help, now desires to eagerly help his father. What better opportunity to walk into. My direct supervisor will be a young man that I truly respect. In addition, I have the honor and privilege of calling him son." Preston smiled as he was finally able to see that his greatest resource toward expanding his business had been standing in front of him.

Motivation in the Moment

God's vision is far greater than we can imagine. When a master plan has been prescribed for you, God will ensure that it is executed precisely. In doing so, it may call for you to be uprooted from where you are today with the ultimate goal of relocating you to somewhere else tomorrow.

In order for God to shed light onto us, sometimes there has to be a subtraction from one part of our lives in order to multiply in others. Although we are often left in a state of disarray, it is then when we have to surrender for guidance. Truly, God has placed us here to prosper. This is evident in the abundance of resources that our surroundings provide. Everything we need is here. We must be willing to open our eyes and grasp the wonderful blessings that often lay at our feet.

Investing in business opportunities with family members promotes a great risk. This is due to the fact that sometimes family issues are often merged into the business arena and vice versa. It is imperative that we analyze in depth the positive and negative aspects of going into business with family members. Sometimes family members are our worst enemy, but they can also function as our most prized asset. As you discern through the utilization of your business mind and not your heart, the answer will definitely surface.

The Awakening

Please respond accordingly.

Question #1

Describe a situation that held grim circumstances that were beyond your realm of influence.

_____

_____

_____

_____

Question #2

How did you attend to it, or what steps are you now taking to attend to it?

_____

_____

_____

_____

Question #3

What lessons did you learn?

_____

_____

_____

_____

CHAPTER 7

Listen to your inner voice. It speaks to you
vibrantly through your feelings. —S. Morrison

Searching for an Understanding

"Charlotte, please! You can't leave like this," Matthew shouted as he stood in front of the door. Still determined, Charlotte tried to reach behind him and grab the doorknob so that she could get out. Charlotte still had not said anything as she stood waiting for Matthew to move out of her way. "What is it? Tell me what I've done, and I'll fix it. Please, I'm begging you. Please don't leave me and the kids like this. Timothy is only one month old. He needs me and you, his mother. Please, Charlotte, don't do this," Matthew stated pleadingly.

As she trembled, Charlotte shouted, "You just don't understand, and I can't explain it! I have to go! Please, let me out!" As she reached for the doorknob after Matthew had finally moved.

He questioned, "Where are you going to go? Can I have a number to call and check on you and let you tell Sabrina that you had to leave?"

As tears swelled in her eyes, she replied, "When I get it together, I will call. I promise. I just have to go." Because he knew something was severely wrong, he did not continue to question her. Before closing the door, Charlotte said, "I will call you." She then closed the door very slowly and softly.

Matthew felt a combination of emotions migrate through his body. He wondered, "What would make a mother just leave her children out of the blue?" He took comfort in feeling that he was a good husband and father. However, he was perplexed over how Charlotte had decided to pack up and leave without any warning. He looked at the clock and discovered that it was now 6:00 pm. It was now time to go and pick up Sabrina from the birthday party she had attended. Matthew quickly grabbed his coat and Timothy, who was already nestled in his car seat, and headed for the door.

When he arrived at Chuck E. Cheese, he marveled at how happy Sabrina looked as she played with her friends. He felt his mood shift as he searched desperately for an appropriate angle to take to explain to Sabrina that her mother had left and that he did not know where she had gone or if she would return.

After noticing her father standing near the video games and holding Timothy in his arms, Sabrina ran to him and stated, "Daddy, Daddy, look what I won." Matthew kneeled down on one knee to see the little purple ring that she wore on her finger. Sabrina questioned, "Where's Mommy?"

Matthew responded, "She couldn't come. We will talk about that a little later. Did you have a good time?"

"Yes," she replied as she hugged Matthew.

"We have to leave now. We have a few errands to run."

"Oh, Daddy, I wanted to play in the balls," she said, as she dropped her little head.

Feeling guilty, Matthew stated, "I will give you five more minutes of play time, but then we have to leave."

"OK, Daddy," she replied, as she hugged Matthew again and then ran to the cage where the balls were.

The next morning as Matthew got Sabrina dressed for school and Timothy ready to go to the babysitter, he felt the effects of his restless night without Charlotte. Because she had been granted a leave of absence to deliver her baby, he knew that she would not have to report to work. Sabrina sat in his lap as he combed her hair. Because she was a daddy's girl, even as an infant, she would only allow Matthew to comb her hair. As a result, getting her dressed for school was a chore that he managed easily. While placing the last barrette in her hair, Sabrina asked, "Daddy, where's Mommy?"

Matthew felt his throat closing. He remained speechless as he searched desperately for an answer. Matthew finally uttered, "Mommy went away for a little while. She said to tell you that she is going to call and let you know when she's coming back."

"Is she OK?" Sabrina asked, as she turned around and faced him.

"Yes, sweetheart," Matthew stated, as he tickled under her arms to distract her. Matthew then said, "While she's gone, she needs you to be a big girl and stay strong until she comes back. Remember, you are Timothy's big sister, and you have to be a good example to him. OK?"

"OK, Daddy," she replied. He hugged Sabrina tightly as she placed her arms around his neck.

Matthew walked into the kitchen, opened the refrigerator, and grabbed a bottle of water. After closing the refrigerator door, he quickly placed it on the kitchen table and grabbed the phone. He dialed, and after the second ring, a soft and brittle voice replied, "Hello."

"Hey, Mom, I just wanted to know if Charlotte was with you. She left yesterday, and I haven't heard from her. I'm a little worried."

"Did you and she have an argument?" Katherine asked. "No," Matthew quickly yet calmly replied.

Katherine stated, "I'm beginning to get worried. She normally calls me and her father every morning, but I haven't heard from her this morning either."

Maintaining his composure but remaining focused, Matthew responded, "It's uncommon for Charlotte to leave and not call."

As she held the telephone tightly to her ear, Katherine continued, "I thought that she was probably a little busy and just hadn't had a chance to call. What did she say before she left?"

"That's the problem. Charlotte didn't say much of anything. She just said she needed to leave," Matthew said. He glanced at the clock on the microwave and discovered that it was now 7:11 am. "Mom, I'm going to have to call you back. I need to get Sabrina to school and drop off Timothy with the babysitter," he stated in a rushed tone.

"I'm sorry for keeping you so long. Just call me later. Matthew, trust me, she will call you. If I hear from her first, I'll make sure that she contacts you," she said tenderly.

"Thank you, Mom," he replied.

After putting on Sabrina's coat, Matthew picked up Timothy in his car seat and headed for the door. The moment Matthew opened the door, Sabrina anxiously walked through it. After closing the door, he heard the phone ring. Matthew grabbed Sabrina's hand and struggled with Timothy's car seat as he opened the door back up. He released Sabrina's hand once they were back inside. Matthew ran for the phone while he tightened the grip on Timothy's car seat. Timothy lay peacefully and unbothered by the quick movements Matthew made as he ran toward the phone.

On the fourth ring, Matthew grabbed the phone. "Hello," Matthew answered hurriedly.

A calm voice stated, "Hello. My name is Dr. Brown. May I please speak with Matthew Fuller?"

"This is Matthew," he quickly responded. Dr. Brown continued, "Mr. Fuller, I'm a physician here at Charter Hospital. Your wife asked me to contact you to inform you that we have admitted her. She is doing well, but we just want to run a few tests on her. You can contact her on her direct line at 870-555-3366."

"Tell her that I'm on my way right now," Matthew quickly responded, as he hung up the phone without saying good-bye.

Matthew's mind was in a frenzy. He immediately called Katherine. On the first ring, a calm voice answered, "Hello."

"Mom, I just heard from Charlotte. She's in the hospital. A doctor from Charter Hospital called and stated that she was OK, but they wanted to run a few tests on her. I'm on my way down there now." He eagerly replied.

Katherine responded, "I'm going to tell her dad, and we'll meet you down there."

Everyone arrived at the hospital and met in the lobby. After the receptionist provided them with Charlotte's room number, they immediately headed to her room. Consumed with anxiety, Matthew and Katherine attempted to console each other as they prepared to enter Charlotte's room to face the unknown. When they entered, Charlotte was sitting in a chair with her hospital gown on, glaring out the window. When she saw Matthew and her mother, she smiled nervously. Matthew quickly rushed over to her. He kissed her and hugged her. Matthew looked her in the eyes and placed her hand in his and said, "We have been worried about you. What's wrong? Did I do something wrong?"

Katherine then hugged her and asked, "Do you need anything, darling?"

Charlotte replied, "Thanks, Mother. But I don't need anything. How are the kids?"

In a comforting tone, Katherine offered, "They're fine. Sabrina was so excited to see her grandfather that she decided to wait downstairs with him and Timothy and allow us to come up and visit you first. Matthew decided to bring them with us when we found out where you were."

Charlotte grinned and paused. She responded, "I'm sorry for causing you to worry. I had to get out. Things were spinning out of control in my mind."

Puzzled, Matthew questioned, "What do mean, Charlotte?"

Charlotte took a deep breath and stated, "I had a feeling growing inside of me that just didn't feel normal. I felt like things were closing in on me, and I needed to do something. Leaving seemed to be the only thing to do before it was too late."

"Charlotte, I don't understand," Matthew quickly yet calmly replied.

Madeline quickly responded, "I understand, darling." She placed her hands gently onto Charlotte's face. She continued, "You have to remember, I'm a mother, too. Trust me. I know exactly what this is." Charlotte felt embarrassment rising within her, but it was immediately aborted as the love in her mother's eyes provided solid evidence of acceptance.

Matthew stated, "Whatever it is, Charlotte, we'll work it out. I just want you to get better, and I'm here to help you." He then smiled at Charlotte as he gently rubbed his hand up and down her arm. Charlotte grinned as she felt the warmth of the love that was surrounding her begin to intensify.

While standing in front of Matthew and staring at Katherine, Charlotte took a deep breath as she took comfort in Katherine's encouraging nod. Charlotte said, "I left so abruptly because a very mysterious feeling overcame me. It became so intense that it terrified me. I knew that it wasn't normal for a mother to have feelings like that toward her son. While bathing Timothy, I had an urge to drown him. I was confused, and I didn't know what to do. I wanted to make him disappear. I felt embarrassed about what I was feeling. Nonetheless, I knew that I needed help immediately. So I decided to leave. It was difficult for me to define what type of help I needed.

When I came here, I was examined by Dr. Brown, and he diagnosed me with postpartum depression. He reassured me that this was something that many women go through after childbirth and that I could be treated with medication. I'm sorry, but the last thing I want to do is harm my children. I would rather leave them than inflict harm on them."

Matthew hugged Charlotte and replied, "Charlotte, you didn't abandon them. You went away to get the help that you knew you needed." Charlotte hugged Matthew even tighter as she saw the light of recovery on the horizon.

Motivation in the Moment

Solutions to very complicated problems can surface in the most ironic form. Some behaviors may be perceived as harmful when examined from one perspective but may be deemed as an act of nobility from another.

God provides us with an inner voice to guide us through our journey. When we are in tune with our inner voice, sometimes those around us may inquire about the reasons for our actions. However, when we are in tune with our inner voice, we are empowered to manage adversity effectively. In some instances, moving aside may allow those things that are meant to come into fruition to surface. Our inner voice communicates with us through our feelings. When we honor our feelings, we are granted an opportunity to discern and conclude on sound decisions.

The Awakening

Please respond accordingly.

Question #1

Can you think of a situation in which you employed a unique problem-solving strategy?

_____

_____

_____

_____

Question #2

What caused you to employ the approach that you took?

_____

_____

_____

_____

Question #3

What did you learn?

_____

_____

_____

_____

CHAPTER 8

Things that seem plain in your eyes are spectacular in the eyes of others. —S. Morrison

Ordinary but Definitely Fabulous

The moment Beverly prepared to enter the gym, butterflies rumbled in her stomach. As she entered, she noticed everyone staring at her. She even caught one of the judges conducting a double take. Beverly walked briskly with her gym bag on her left shoulder, and her own flagpole tucked tightly under her right armpit. She held the strap on her gym bag so tight that her hands had begun to sweat. She walked toward Jonathan and slipped him the CD that she had convinced him to play when her number was called. Secretly concealed within her bag, she possessed the ammunition she needed to execute her plan of attack.

After receiving her number, Beverly walked toward the first open seat that she saw. But Beverly had to pass by the "Ice Princesses," which included Melissa, Athena, and Jaqueline, who were very close friends. They had earned this nickname because they were very pretty, but they were also cold and cruel to others. Because of their similar mannerisms and appearance, they were often mistaken as sisters. Nonetheless, they were ranked among the top tier in regard to their social status at Douglas High School.

They had returned to the audition to assume their reserved positions on the flag line. Because Athena was graduating, Melissa was looking forward to moving from being co-captain to becoming captain. This would give Jaqueline the opportunity to become the new co-captain. As Beverly passed, she heard Athena, who acted as the informal president of their clique state, "What is she doing here? I thought she didn't make it through the first audition? Why does she have all of that stuff?" Athena laughed, causing Jaqueline and Melissa to laugh as well. Beverly refused to acknowledge them. She was able to ignore them by maintaining her focus on what lay ahead of her.

Unfortunately, somehow she became infected with the negativity that was directed toward her. After hearing Athena's statement, Beverly silently questioned why she had come to the second round of the audition. She glanced over at Jonathan, and he smiled. His smile provided her with the encouragement that she needed greatly. It gave her the confidence to complete the audition.

Beverly saw the audition as an opportunity to make a commitment to complete a task and see it through. Because she was voluptuous, becoming a cheerleader or a member of the track team was definitely out of the question. In addition, she would not consider the thought of attending the tryouts for the volleyball and basketball teams because she disliked those sports.

Beverly thought about all the measures that she had gone through to prepare for her audition. She knew that it was too late to back out of the audition. No matter what, she had to do it. She refused to let anyone see how nervous she was. She conducted a quick mental review of all that she had done in preparation for her audition.

Beverly had her father purchase a metal pole from Home Depot, and she had persuaded her mother to purchase fabric to make a flag to attach to the pole. This makeshift flag suited her perfectly when she needed to practice her routine in the event that she made it through the first round of audition cuts. She even enlisted the assistance of Mrs. Nan, an elderly neighbor, to assist with the outfit that she wanted to wear.

Beverly watched nervously as each candidate moved through their routine. As each minute sluggishly passed and her number moved closer to being called, she felt nausea climb within her. When she discovered she had only one person ahead of her, Beverly began to perspire heavily. She held the strap of her gym bag tightly in her right hand as the bag lay on the floor between her legs.

The tension that she felt would have been eliminated if it were not for the fact that she had to audition after Jaqueline. When Jaqueline began her audition, Beverly rushed to the locker room to get prepared. She reached in her bag and pulled out the gold satin blouse, the first piece of her uniform. After putting it on, she was reassured of her decision to wear it since it served as a perfect complement to the navy blue skirt, with a gold stripe that lay perfectly on each side.

As she put on the metallic gold eye shadow and the blue glitter on her face, she smiled as she reflected upon Mrs. Nan saying, "You have to think of yourself as a soldier. They wear paint on their faces to blend into the background. You have to do the same to show them that you can blend into the background with the rest of the girls on the squad. This is not just a battle, this is war. You need to wear your war paint, which is your makeup." Beverly smiled as she pulled her hair back into a ponytail and put on the navy blue cowboy hat that had a gold ribbon stitched around it. As she looked at herself in the mirror, she witnessed the excellent job Mrs. Nan had done in creating a perfect replica of the school's uniform. Beverly knew she would become the next complement to epitomize the Lancer pride at Douglas High School.

Beverly stood in the doorway of the locker room waiting for her number to be called. She leaned up against the wall with her arms folded as she went over her entire routine in her mind. When she glanced down at her feet, she smiled as she was provided with another silent reminder of Mrs. Nan. The old white boots that had once belonged to Mrs. Nan's daughter twenty years ago had a fresh application of white shoe polish, which highlighted the large navy blue and gold tassels that Mrs. Nan had sewn onto them. Suddenly, Beverly heard "Number 36." Beverly's concentration was broken as she quickly responded, "Ready." Jonathan heard his cue and then began the music. Although she ran the risk of being disqualified for manipulating the audition music, she knew her music would provide the impact that she desired.

The music started, and Beverly tucked her flagpole under her armpit so that it would drape behind her. She bowed her head and grabbed the brim of her hat. She exhaled a deep breath and waited for her cue of the whistle blowing on the Outkast's song entitled "Morris Brown." When Beverly heard her cue, "Tweeeeeeeeeet ... tweet, tweet, tweet," she balled her left hand and placed it on her hip as she shook them from left to right on each blow of the whistle. The song began with the vibrant beat of the percussion section accompanied by the tuba section. Beverly was careful not to let anyone see her until she gracefully launched herself from the locker room. Before anyone could respond to the music being compromised, everyone focused on the homemade uniform she wore as she trotted along the wall and continued under the basketball goal. Once she arrived there, she made a left flank and continued trotting until she was in the center of the gym. Beverly heard the muffled laughs, but she refused to allow the laughter to distract her. She made another left flank as the music jump cut to "Here I Come" by Fergie, which was a perfect fit to announce her arrival.

When the music changed, she noticed the laughter had begun to climb even higher. As fear consumed her, Beverly remained headstrong as she noticed two of the judges glance at each other and smile. She just hoped they would not interrupt the audition because of what she was wearing and convincing Jonathan to alter the audition music.

At that moment, Beverly was unaware that they were only admiring her choice of music because the track to "Here I Come" was a remixed track to "Get Ready" by the Temptations. Two of the judges, as former members of the Prancing J-settes of Jackson State University, could not help being taken on a very fond nostalgic journey to when the band played this song as they danced to it.

After arriving at her desired spot, Beverly turned her back to the judges, spread her legs, and then bowed her head. She waited three seconds and then moved flawlessly through the routine that she was taught the previous day at the audition. She left everyone in awe as she lifted her left leg and twirled the flag under it and then threw it into the air and caught it. She then twirled it behind her back and rotated her body from front to back. Although these two moves were not part of the audition routine, she felt the impact of these moves would capture the attention of the judges.

The blouse that she wore hugged her perfectly, and her skirt accented her young, voluptuous yet budding physique in every move she made. Beverly's appearance projected a very strong and charismatic aura that was immediately detected by the judges and the "Ice Princesses." In the middle of the routine, she dropped to the floor and began twirling the flag on her back. While lying there, she rotated the flag between her legs. Although she stood the risk of being disqualified for adding this move as well, she wanted everyone to realize that although she was overweight, she was limber and possessed a lot of stamina.

Beverly then transitioned to another move in which she tossed the flag into the air and then caught it behind her back as she faced forward. Everyone glared and remained speechless. As Beverly recognized this, Beverly's adrenaline climbed even higher as she concluded her routine with two high kicks and dropped to the floor into a split with a salute to the judges.

When she finished the routine, the room remained silent. With anger in her eyes, Athena looked at Jacqueline and Melissa and asked, "Which one of you helped her with that routine? Someone on this squad had to help her." Puzzled, Jacqueline and Melissa looked at each other as they searched desperately to discover the culprit who had broken the bond of their now shaky friendship.

While she moved through her routine, Beverly discovered that it really did not matter if she made the squad. She discovered that she had accomplished something far greater than making the squad.

Beverly knew she had accomplished her mission because she had made a concentrated effort to audition and she had withstood her self-doubt. Indeed, through her actions, she had liberated herself from her self-doubt. With the payoff of heightened confidence, it really did not matter whether she was disqualified or made the squad. Through her willingness to overcome these obstacles, the victory was hers.

As Beverly walked toward the exit, she passed Jacqueline, Melissa, and Athena with a smile that showed her humility. Beverly knew that saying anything derogatory in regard to what she overheard would be fruitless at this point. The achievement and excellence that was displayed in the execution of her routine was enough payback for the insensitive statements directed toward her. Beverly had declared war on an advanced level, and the victory was hers. The extra effort that she had taken to create her own uniform and modify the audition routine only made the judges aware of how serious she was.

On the next day, footage from the audition was recorded by one of the other candidates on their cell phone and uploaded to YouTube in an effort to make a mockery of her. To her aggressor's dismay, Beverly's hard work did not go unrecognized. When the results were posted, Beverly did not secure a spot on the flag line as member of the squad, but she was selected to be the new co-captain. It was the first time in the history of the school in which a candidate bumped an incumbent out of a position of leadership.

Motivation in the Moment

Our flaws are truly relative. On many occasions, our flaws can function as an asset for us. Because we are our own worst critic, we have a tendency to make reference to our flaws in a negative manner. However, when our flaws are uncovered by others, our greatest flaws can often function as our most prized asset in the eyes of others.

When we take the time and energy to understand our flaws, we can truly gain an understanding of the hidden blessings that reside in them. Often we are introduced to our flaws at an early age. In some cases, they may have been magnified by those that we love the most. However, we must conduct a self-assessment to gain an understanding of the greatness that resides in each of us. We may seem flawed to the naked eye, but we are an image of perfection which was created precisely the way God intended. Because God is love, it is truly important for us to love and cherish who we are.

The Awakening

Please respond accordingly.

Question #1

What flaws do you think you have?

_____

_____

_____

_____

Question #2

Did you bring attention to your flaws or did someone else?

_____

_____

_____

_____

Question #3

Describe an occasion when someone embraced one of your worst flaws in a positive manner.

_____

_____

_____

_____

CHAPTER 9

A cycle of despair and hopelessness that has been passed down for generations can be broken starting with you.—S. Morrison

Not Like You

"Go ahead, Iris, drink it. I know you'll like the taste of it," Celeste stated. Iris began to feel uneasy as she sat in the backseat of the car. She slowly raised the cup to her mouth and gently placed her lips on the rim of the cup. The distasteful smell of the liquor solidified her decision not to drink it. Thoughts raced through her mind as she attempted to capture an idea of how she could find another way to fit in. Iris felt as though this was her only and last chance to be accepted by Celeste, Mitchell, and Yolanda.

Earlier in the night, she was able to convince Yolanda that she had asthma to avoid smoking marijuana with them. Nonetheless, Iris felt that if she was going to fit in with the popular crowd, she would be obligated to do everything everyone else did. Suddenly, Iris felt a cold chill move through her. Drug and alcohol addiction stood as two dominating forces within her family. She thought about how easily she could become like those closest to her. After her quick assessment, Iris decided not to take the risk of flirting with alcohol and possibly being held hostage under its spell.

Iris quickly concluded that the cost of acceptance from her peers was suddenly no longer important to her. She had set goals for herself, and failure was not an option for her. Furthermore, she felt that she needed a clear mind to get through the grim reality that had held her captive for so long.

Iris grabbed her cell phone and looked at her display and stated, "I need to get home immediately. My mother just sent me a text message stating that she wants me to come home right now." Iris then passed the cup back. She then continued, "Dang! I really wanted to hang out with you guys, but I better get home soon. Mitchell, would you please drop me off?"

Mitchell quickly responded, "We're almost at the mall."

"Don't be so difficult, Mitchell! Just drop her off. She has to get home," Celeste barked at Mitchell. Iris smiled as she realized Celeste believed this lie as well.

After arriving home, Iris walked into the dimly lit but well decorated living room and was greeted by the sweet but tainted odor that dominated the room. Her father, Milford, lay asleep on the couch, passed out as usual. Both he and Iris' mother, Evelyn, had missed another day of work because they had a hangover and had overslept.

Evelyn sat motionless in a chair in the corner of the living room. Iris entered the living room and dryly said, "Hi, Mom." Iris quickly headed toward her bedroom. After taking a few steps past Evelyn, Iris felt a bizarre tug on her arm which resulted in her being jerked backward and brought her eye to eye with Evelyn.

"You can't speak? Where have you been?" Evelyn questioned commandingly.

"I did speak. I spoke the moment I entered the room. I went over to Celeste's house to get a book that I needed for an assignment in our history class," Iris quickly responded.

"No, you didn't!" Evelyn stated, as she folded her arms. She then peered into Iris' eyes mercilessly, coercing Iris to silently acknowledge Evelyn's bloodshot eyes.

"If you are going to continue to live here, you are going to have to learn to show more respect toward the directions that your father and I provide. When school ends, the only stop that you are allowed to make is here, at home." Evelyn stated forcefully.

"Yes, ma'am. I apologize. May I go to my room now?" Iris asked, as Evelyn continued her motionless stare. After a few moments of silence, Evelyn moved out of the way and allowed Iris to pass by her.

After entering her bedroom, Iris angrily threw her backpack onto the bed. She threw it so hard that it bounced off the bed and hit the wall. Several moments later Evelyn burst through the bedroom door. "Do you have something you want to say to me? The way that you are slamming things around in here says that you do." Evelyn stated as she briskly approached Iris and slapped her across her right cheek and then grabbed her by her throat.

Evelyn slapped Iris so hard that her brother Cameron heard it in his bedroom, causing him to leave his bedroom and stand outside her door. Tears swelled in Iris' eyes as the red handprint on her face reassured Iris that she had become a participant in another episode of Evelyn's meaningless confrontations while drunk.

As in the past, Iris knew exactly what to do to end the confrontation. She knew that her mother thrived off of fear. Iris allowed her tears to glaze her face. After sensing her fear, Evelyn stated, "No one slams things around in this house but me and your father. We have the right to get upset around here." After a few seconds of silence, while still standing there in her mother's grip, Iris felt a thump inside. It was foreign to her, and it caused her to feel guilty. Iris stood with her arms dangling at her sides.

Unlike the many times before, Iris had balled her fists and was preparing to strike back at her mother. Without notice, Evelyn released Iris' neck from her death grip and walked out of the bedroom. Iris knew that physical confrontations like this could not continue. She began to cry harder. There was a knock at her bedroom door. "Come in," Iris said softly.

Cameron entered Iris' bedroom and asked, "Are you OK?"

Iris replied, "I'm fine." She pushed her hair out of her face which provided Cameron with an opportunity to discover the tears that she had shed. Ironically, the tears that Iris shed on this occasion were not tears of fear; they were tears of aggravation.

Cameron sat on the bed next to Iris and placed his arm around her and hugged her consolingly. He said, "Don't cry, Iris. It's going to get better." He exhaled after taking a deep breath, and then released a very light chuckle and stated, "You're graduating at the end of this school year, and you will be on your way out of here. I'm stuck here for another year before I can leave." Iris smiled as she leaned her head on Cameron's shoulder, as the soothing warmth of his words and warm affection eased her aching soul.

Iris was concerned because of her urge to strike her mother. Because she respected her mother, she refused to attack her. Nonetheless, she acknowledged the fact that if Evelyn continued to attack her, it would not be long before they would engage in a fistfight.

In an attempt to bring peace to her situation, Iris made it a point to do everything to stay off of her mother's path. During the next four months, Iris went the extra mile to finish her daily chores, while continuing to maintain her good grades. Even though this was her senior year of high school and it was supposed to be the best year of her life, it was the worst of many. The abuse that she had endured over the years had become excessive and intolerable.

Iris felt as though she was a time bomb patiently waiting to go off. Even though she was very young, Iris was capable of acknowledging this fact and was capable of putting corrective measures in motion. Iris decided that she would work a part-time job at McDonald's. The job would keep her out of the house during the evenings and weekends. As she had planned, Iris was able to limit her interaction even further with her mother.

The months dragged, but graduation day had finally arrived. During the ceremony, Iris looked into the audience to locate her parents. She finally discovered Cameron, but he was sitting by himself. When their eyes met, Iris smiled as she saw Cameron's explosive smile on his face as he waived hysterically. His actions reminded her of how much he truly adored her.

Iris waived back as she tried to hold back the tears of disappointment that consumed her. She knew that her parents were probably out on a drinking binge. She immediately resolved her dismay about her parents' absence by being thankful that Cameron was there. His presence represented love, and at that moment, that was all Iris needed.

After the graduation ceremony, Iris went to a graduation party with Simone, a new acquaintance she had begun to hang out with. It was approximately 12:31 am when Iris arrived home. She unlocked the front door and entered the dark living room. After taking two steps, Iris turned and closed the door. "Whack!" "Whack!" Suddenly, Iris felt a sharp pain penetrate her back and spine that quickly caused her to become disoriented. "You're not going to disrespect my home by staying out late!" Evelyn yelled, as she jumped from behind the door and hit Iris again with the broom.

"You can't come into my house at any hour of the night! I know that you were probably out messing around with some boy you probably met on the street! You're a tramp, and you don't have me fooled! Iris, if you get pregnant, I'm not raising any more children! Not only that, you are going to have to get out of my house!" Evelyn yelled vehemently. Iris turned around and faced Evelyn. Peering into her mother's dark eyes with a very cold stare was the only way to conceal the pain that she felt inside from being called promiscuous, when she was still a virgin. The sting of her mother's words injured her more than being hit by the broom. Iris searched for an answer as to why her mother would say such cruel things to her.

During their silent standoff, in a quick moment, Iris was finally able to understand and accept her reality. Iris reflected on how her mother had always been cruel to her. Evelyn's rage provided another opportunity to reveal the true person that she had always been.

Assertively, yet stiff and emotionless, Iris stated, "I apologize for disrespecting your home by coming home after midnight. I can assure you, Mother, that it won't ever happen again." Iris walked rigidly to her bedroom. As she entered her bedroom, she saw Cameron standing in the hall with a worried look on his face. Iris calmly said, "I'm fine, Cameron. Go back to bed." Cameron lowered his head and slowly stepped back into his bedroom and then quietly closed his door. Iris went into her bedroom and closed her door.

As she started to take off her dress, Iris' bedroom door suddenly burst open. "I'm not finished with you yet, you tramp!" Evelyn yelled, as she swung the broom at Iris. Successfully, Iris obstructed the blow that her mother intended to impose upon her by grabbing the broom with both hands.

Without any struggle, Iris took the broom from Evelyn and stated, "You are finished with me! That's it, Mother! I won't allow you to just beat on me without a reason." Iris went to her closet and opened it. She pulled out the bags that she had packed. She then went under her bed and pulled out the boxes that she had packed and a few other items that she would need.

Irritably, Evelyn stated, "Where are you going?"

Calmly, Iris replied, "I've been accepted into Washington University. Since I'm going to major in math, I was granted an opportunity to participate in the summer math program which is scheduled to end two weeks before the fall semester begins. The university has assisted me with subletting an apartment for the summer until I can move into the dormitory in the fall. I didn't tell you sooner because I knew that you would attempt to discourage me by telling me what a failure I am."

The vein on Evelyn's forehead emerged, which provided solid evidence of how angry she had become. "You think that you're better than us. Don't you?" Evelyn barked. Unbothered, Iris refused to respond as she continued to stack the boxes on her bed. "Good. Well, don't call us for any help. You're on your own. You'll be back," she stated, as she laughed sarcastically and left Iris' room.

The next morning at 7:30 am Evelyn opened Iris' bedroom door only to discover an empty room with a note with her contact information.

"She left early this morning. Iris said to tell you that she was sorry that she had to leave like this, but she knew it would be better. She used the money she saved from working to purchase her plane ticket and to get herself set up. She promised to call once she has gotten settled," Cameron offered, as he witnessed Evelyn reading the note. He took comfort in the fact that Iris had finally left for college.

Cameron had become even more excited over the fact that Iris had made a secret promise to him that morning that she would assist him in getting accepted so that he could come and join her. If things continued to get bad for him, Iris reassured him that she would move out of the dormitory and get an apartment so that he could come live with her and finish his last year of high school.

Evelyn felt defeat coloring her mood like a shadow of darkness, especially after reading the closing of the letter. Iris wrote, *I love you Mother, but I love you enough to leave and love you from a distance.* The distance that Iris had placed between her and Evelyn would function as a healing tool to mend their fragile and dysfunctional relationship.

As a result of Iris' departure, Evelyn became riddled with guilt as she reflected and embraced the reality that had she, too, been like Iris and stood up to her mother, she could have captured the dreams that lay broken and tucked away in yesterday.

Motivation in the Moment

When an obstruction is placed on our path, maintaining focus on our prescribed goals can be extremely challenging. It is true that parents can say and do cruel things that can in some instances dismantle our self-esteem. Although our independent circumstances can vary in the types of complications that we encounter, we must acknowledge the reality of the fact that each of us is responsible for creating a tomorrow which incorporates hope and promise for ourselves. We are commissioned to unlock the opportunities that are present in today, as well as those silently tucked away in tomorrow.

It is our duty to persistently challenge ourselves to think creatively when dealing with adversity. Within our creative energy reside the solutions to some of life's more complicated moments. Education is a key to opportunity. It unlocks realities with unlimited possibilities. Higher education can provide a remedy to complicated circumstances. Truly, it is a strategic step toward independence, especially when your livelihood is sustained by others.

The Awakening

Please respond accordingly.

Question #1
What personality traits do you find most disturbing about your parents that you hope not to continue?

_____

_____

_____

_____

Question #2
What coping mechanisms do you employ?

_____

_____

_____

_____

Question #3
Describe an occasion in which you were able to utilize conflict as a stepping-stone toward success.

_____

_____

_____

_____

CHAPTER 10

Everyone serves a function in your life. When those in your life have satisfied their purpose in your journey, circumstances will surface which will cause them to exit. —S. Morrison

Good-bye Now and Forever

"Carl, you know that I'm your friend," Nemesis stated pleadingly. "If this is your idea of being a good friend to me, I can't afford to have you as an enemy. I can't believe this is happening to me," Carl blurted, as he palmed the center of his head with his left hand, and then slammed the glass of wine he held in his right hand down on the table. As the wine flowed freely onto the table and the hundreds of pieces of glass scattered across it, Carl saw the first symbolic projection of his severed ties with Nemesis.

"After fourteen years of friendship, is this how it ends for us, Nemesis?" Carl questioned as he felt his insides begin to throb with anger. The tightened muscles in his face magnified his anger as he looked into Nemesis' dark and cold eyes.

"I really don't have time for this. This is foolish," Nemesis stated, indicating that he was unbothered by what Carl had said. Nemesis grabbed his briefcase and walked out the door. Once outside, Nemesis did not bother to turn around because he knew that this was indeed a chapter of his life that had been officially closed.

After closing the door, Carl turned and knocked down the mahogany statue that stood peacefully on the pedestal next to the door. Every inch of Carl's body and mind became consumed with guilt, sadness, and anger. Nonetheless, he felt that Nemesis' decision to leave was probably the most appropriate thing he could do. After hearing what he had heard, there was nothing left for Carl to do but to confront Nemesis about his actions from the previous night.

The night before was picture perfect for the album release party that Arista Records was hosting for Carl, who had just recently signed with them, and was officially launching his new album entitled "Epiphany of a Perfect Love." The excitement associated with the evening enlivened Carl which was evident in his smile which lit up the room.

Finally, all of the work that he had done over the last ten years had paid off. Singing as a backup singer for Sire, Brittany Spears, Justin Timberlake, and Ne-Yo had prepared him for the greatness that lay ahead in his immediate future. Time had finally presented Carl with an opportunity to step into the spotlight as a solo artist. Since Carl wanted the party to be classified as a marketing masterpiece, he even requested that Kesha Monks, the radio personality from New York City's 98.7 FM, serve as his hostess for the evening.

Because of the euphoria associated with the evening, Carl had consumed a high level of water, alcohol, and soda, which had caused him to pay frequent visits to the restroom. As the evening progressed and the night came to a close, he went into the restroom not only to use it but also to just take a small break from all of the excitement. While in the restroom stall, he propped his legs up so that no one could see him. After sitting there a few moments, Carl heard a familiar voice speaking on his cell phone as he entered the restroom. The voice stated, "I think this party was OK. It definitely could've been a lot better. I don't know how much longer I'm going to be around. I'm growing a little tired of dealing with amateur productions. As a matter of fact, I'm searching for new career opportunities as we speak. The moment an opportunity arises for me to manage another artist, I'm going to resign as his manager." As his mouth fell open, Carl noticed that the voice he heard sounded familiar. The voice continued, "I'm doing just enough work to get me by. I'm looking forward to working with more of a top-notch artist." The voice then exhaled a very frigid and sinister laugh as he grabbed three paper towels from the dispenser. After retrieving them, he immediately left the restroom.

Carl felt a cold chill come over him as he quickly recognized the voice. Carl froze as his mind searched to discover a reason why his friend and manager, Nemesis, had turned against him. Carl felt numb as he journeyed through his mind and recaptured their fourteen-year friendship. He remembered how Nemesis was instrumental in introducing him to Gabriel, who signed him with Arista Records.

Because of his support and ties within the record industry, Carl felt that Nemesis would be a perfect manager. Carl's stomach rumbled as he thought about the countless times that Nemesis supported his efforts. Disappointment mounted within him as Carl revisited the occasion when Nemesis loaned him money to purchase studio time to record his demo to submit to the record company.

Carl became paralyzed, but he knew that he had to attend to this matter whether he liked it or not. After Nemesis left the restroom, Carl waited ten minutes before leaving. After exiting the restroom and as he approached the crowd he heard, "Carl! Come over here for a minute." When Carl turned, he displayed a look of disgust on his face when he discovered that it was Nemesis who was calling his name. As he walked toward Nemesis, he felt a sudden urge to punch Nemesis in the mouth. However, if he did that, Carl knew that it would only leave a horrible impression on his guests, and it could diminish his reputation as a new artist. Carl quickly felt that the best way to address the situation was to paint a smile on his face. He frigidly approached Nemesis.

"Yes?" He replied with a plastic smile, as he awaited Nemesis' response.

Nemesis said, "I want to introduce you to Michael Thomas. He's a director, and he's interested in directing your first video. Because he's excited about the possibility of working with you, he's willing to shoot the video at a very low promotional rate."

Extending his arm, Carl replied, "It's a pleasure to meet you."

"Here is my card. I would really like to work with you. Please give me a call next week," Michael eagerly stated.

Carl quickly responded, "I sure will."

"Hey, that's my job," Nemesis interrupted and turned to Michael and then exhaled a very light chuckle. Nemesis tried to take the business card that Carl refused to release. Feeling a little embarrassed, Nemesis stated, "We'll definitely meet next week."

Carl thought, *This fool is an ambassador for the devil. Sabotaging my career and our friendship have become two full-time jobs. He couldn't possibly have any free time on his hands to do anything else.* Carl tightened his already fixed smile and then quickly responded, "I will definitely be in touch with you soon." Carl shook Michael's hand and resumed mingling with his guests.

Carl maintained his composure and made it through the evening. The next morning Carl awoke and lay in bed in the dark bedroom, playing back the entire evening in his mind. He found himself immobilized in regard to having to deal with Nemesis. Because he was faced with this new awareness in regard to Nemesis, he needed to take action fast.

Carl reached for his phone and dialed Nemesis' number. After the third ring, Nemesis answered, "Good morning, Mr. Superstar. How are you?"

"I'm fine," Carl replied pleasantly. Through his plastic greeting Carl concluded that his phone number was displayed on Nemesis' caller ID. Carl continued, "Nemesis, I need to meet with you to discuss a few things. Let's meet at my house about 8:00 pm."

"No problem. I'll see you then," Nemesis replied. Carl hung up the phone. He was so irritated that it took the entire day to shower, get dressed, and collect his thoughts. Although an entire day had passed, it seemed as if Carl had just ended their call, and then the door bell immediately rang. After the second ring, Carl answered the door. As he opened the door, it happened again. This time the urge to punch Nemesis had grown even higher, especially due to the fact that there would be no one to witness a fistfight if they engaged in one.

As Carl slowly opened the door, Nemesis quickly said, "Hey, Carl. How are you?" Nemesis placed his hand on the door to open it wider, inviting himself in.

"I'm fine. Thanks for asking," Carl stated, as he worked desperately to maintain his pleasant demeanor. In doing so, Carl discovered that he was sweating heavily. As the anger throbbed within him, a voice inside of him kept urging Carl to punch Nemesis in the mouth. Thankfully, the voice of reason spoke at a level and a tone which prevented Carl from doing so.

"What did you think about last night? Wasn't it awesome? Everything turned out exactly as we planned," Nemesis stated, as he headed toward the kitchen to help himself to a bottle of water in the refrigerator. Nemesis spoke so fast that Carl could not get a word in to answer the questions that he asked. Unaware that Carl had not responded, Nemesis continued, "I told you that you didn't have anything to worry about. You are definitely making a name for yourself. Now we need to move to the next step. We need to discuss your music video." Nemesis sat down at the kitchen table and pulled out his Blackberry and put it on top of the folder that he had placed upon the table.

"Stop it, Nemesis! Cut it out! We're not here to discuss the music video. I need to confront you about your lackluster performance as my manager and your betrayal of me as a friend," Carl stated forcefully.

Puzzled, Nemesis looked at Carl and stated, "I don't understand what you're saying."

Carl felt the anger move through him and then yelled, "You know exactly what I mean, Nemesis! Don't sit there and look as if you haven't done anything to injure me."

Maintaining his perplexed demeanor, Nemesis responded, "I'm lost, Carl. What do you mean stating that my performance as your manager has been lackluster? How did I betray you as a friend?"

Carl violently pushed the folder on which Nemesis had placed his Blackberry. The papers flew in one direction while the folder and the Blackberry flew in another. Carl stated, "Well, let me spell it out for you, Nemesis. I heard everything you said about me last night when you were in the restroom. That's right. You're busted! As of this moment, you are officially released of duty as my manager, and our ties as friends are dissolved."

Nemesis sat motionless for a few moments. He replied, "Apparently you're upset about something, and you need time to clear your mind. I think you just need a little space. So I'll just give you a call in a couple of days." Nemesis quickly rose from the table and collected the paperwork that lay on the kitchen floor along with his Blackberry.

Carl felt a mysterious calmness come over him. As he watched Nemesis collect the paperwork on the floor, he remained silent. Feeling embarrassed, Nemesis quickly headed toward the front door. As he stood there alone, Carl looked at the pieces of the broken statue, he felt that it too was symbolic of the broken bonds of their personal and professional ties. As Carl walked into the kitchen, he concentrated on the bottle of unopened water that Nemesis had placed on the table. At that moment, Carl became awakened to the metaphorical meaning of the water and their friendship. The transparent quality provided evidence of Nemesis actions. Carl was completely unaware that the bonds of their friendship had shifted and had soured. The reality that Carl faced presented him with factual evidence. Although he was sullen, Carl was thankful for the new lesson that Nemesis taught him. He accepted the fact that he was coerced into saying good-bye to someone whom he had loved and trusted. However, God, along with the tenderness of time, would eventually present an opportunity to provide an introduction to someone who possessed the characteristics worthy of being called a friend. He now understood the importance of accepting the reality that mastering good-bye would now and forever become an integral component in his journey.

Motivation in the Moment

As we move through many of the high and low points of our spiritual journey, saying good-bye is an element which is definitely associated with moving to the next dimension. Although we find it difficult to say good-bye to those who once functioned as anchors in the form of nurture and support, it is a reality that we must learn to acknowledge and accept. Indeed, we hope that our kind acts are reciprocated by those who we bestowed them upon.

It is human nature for the kindness and love that we graciously extend to others to be returned to us. Whether we like it or not, it is also a part of human nature for someone to be loved and nurtured by us and then later harm us. Truly, embracing a reality such as this in some instances can become crippling. Nonetheless, we must remember that we are imperfect, and God recognizes this. He grants mercy upon us in the form of strategically aligning our lives with someone else to maintain the circular flow of the acts of kindness. Always remember that God is truly an awesome God.

The Awakening

Question #1
Describe an occasion when you felt betrayed.

_____

_____

_____

_____

Question #2
What did you do to cope with your situation?

_____

_____

_____

_____

Question #3
What can you take away from this experience that would function as a learning tool?

_____

_____

_____

_____

EPILOGUE

There is a light that shines vibrantly in each of us. However, many of us experience difficulty seeing our light. This is due to the fact that our light shines so brightly that it blinds us, but it functions as a guide to those around us.

I encourage you to continue to be a light for those who surround you since they may be a light for you. Nonetheless, it is our duty to take the responsibility of being our own beacon of light in the gloom and darkness of adversity. As life presents circumstances that are grim and dreadful, take the time to acknowledge how you feel and recognize the importance of moving forward with your journey. In honoring exactly how you feel, you become equipped to put corrective measures in place to activate the charismatic dynamism that resides in each of us.

During the course of each day, God presents us with many opportunities to ignite our light so that we can expand upon our spiritual growth. From this, we are then left with the ability to utilize what we learn. As we apply what we internalize from these experiences, we then provide solid evidence that application is mastery of the highest level of learning.

Coming Soon:

Signatures of Inspiration

Available Resources

Alzheimer's Association
1-800-272-3900
alz.org

Project Inform-AIDS/HIV
1-800-822-7422
hivinsite.ucsf.edu
projectinform.org

Centers for Disease Control and Prevention
1-800-CDC-INFO
cdc.gov

National Domestic Violence Hotline
1-800-799-SAFE (7233)
ndvh.org

Also by Steven D. Morrison

stevendmorrison.com
Price: $10.95
ISBN-10: 0595380344
ISBN-13: 978-0595380343

ARTEMIS CONSULTING GROUP

Reach Greater Heights!

Our interactive workshops cover a number of
key areas in workplace development.

- Team-Building Strategies

- Management Training

- Conflict/Resolution in the
  Workplace

- Sexual Harassment Training

- Managing Change in the
  Workplace

- Diversity Training

- Creating an Individual
  Development Plan

- Mastering Phone Etiquette

- Career Development

- Leadership Development

- Customer Relationship
  Management

- Stress Management

- Assertiveness Development

- Life/Work Balance

- Setback Management

- Workplace Violence

- Professionalism in the
  Workplace

We offer the following services based upon specific demand.

- Special Event Speaking
- Train-the-Trainer
- Résumé Writing
- Customized workshops for any specified area of interest

Artemis Consulting Group, LLC
Department 3A
P.O. Box 83449
Atlanta, GA 30013
404-664-4769
info@ArtemisConsultingGroup.net
ArtemisConsultingGroup.net

LaVergne, TN USA
24 September 2009
158895LV00004B/28/P